PICK
MONL

Optimize Your Game With Analytics

© Tim Swartz, PhD

Burnaby, 2025

Foreward

Dr. Swartz is a pioneer in sports analytics who has devoted much of his career to the application of statistics and computation in sport. He has produced seminal work across various sports at a technical level. This monograph is a departure for him as he brings insights involving the sport of pickleball to the general public.

The strategies that he suggests are interesting, well-explained and well-argued. There is also a touch of humor in his writing. I think that many people are going to enjoy this book. It is the most original and thought-provoking contribution on pickleball that is out there.

Professor MJ
Sports Handicapper

Professor MJ's sports betting tips and winning systems can be seen on his YouTube channel; go to MJPicks.com

Acknowledgments

There are a number of people that I would like to thank who had a hand in the genesis of this book. I want to spread the love in six directions.

First, I would like to thank my wife Kim. Having entered the latter stages of my career, Kim has advised me that I should now start doing projects that I really want to do. She said, why don't you write another book? Do something less technical where you can write to a broad audience. You love pickleball - why don't you write about pickleball? So, we brainstormed, and Kim had many good ideas. So, this is where the book began. Kim has always been supportive of my career.

Second, I would like to thank my eldest daughter Philippa. She has a BSc and an MSc in Statistics, and also a JD degree (Law). But these days, Philippa refers to herself as an entrepreneur, and engages in various internet businesses. She has vetted the book (from the perspective of a person who does not play pickleball). She has also contributed greatly to design, production and marketing, all things that I know little about.

Third, I would like to thank Dr. Paramjit Gill of the University of British Columbia, Okanagan. He is recently retired, and is my longtime collaborator on all sorts of projects. I have written more papers with Paramjit than with anyone else. Paramjit got into pickleball earlier than me; he plays every day. And together we wrote the first technical journal article on pickleball.[1] Paramjit's role in this book was as a reviewer, from the perspective of a pickleball player who is an expert in Statistics.

---

[1] Gill, P.S. and Swartz, T.B. (2019). A characterization of the degree of weak and strong links in doubles sports. Journal of Quantitative Analysis in Sports, 15, 155-162.

Fourth, I would like to thank Rick Stevens who served as the third reviewer. He reviewed the book from the perspective of a smart person who is an avid pickleball player but does not have formal training in Statistics. I relied on Rick to help make the book more accessible.

Fifth, I would like to thank Mahen Muthukumarana. Mahen is responsible for most of the figures produced in the book. Mahen is an undergraduate Statistics student at Simon Fraser University (SFU), Canada. Typically, I only work with MSc and PhD students, but Mahen is different. First, he is very clever. Second, I have known him since he was a baby. I was the supervisor of both of his parents, Saman and Aruni, who were graduate students at SFU. They came to Canada from Sri Lanka. Aruni works as a researcher in medical statistics at the University of Manitoba where Saman is now Chair and Professor in the Department of Statistics.

And sixth, I would like to thank the Pickleball Club at Country Roads RV Village in Yuma, Arizona. This is where my wife and I go to vacation and for me to play pickleball during the Canadian winters. The club has more than 350 players; they are a welcoming community and they make the game fun.

Thank you all.

Contents

I INTRODUCTION　　1

1 Pickleball and the Book　　2
   1.1 A Brief History of Pickleball 2
   1.2 Evolution in Sport 4
   1.3 Motivation 10

2 The Rules of Pickleball　　14

3 The Pillars of Pickleball　　19
   3.1 Skill 20
   3.2 Athleticism 21
   3.3 Strategy 22
   3.4 Luck 24

II MUSINGS ON STRATEGY　　27

4 Parking the Bus　　29
   4.1 Cautious Play in Pickleball 31

5 Approaching the Net　　37

6 The Banger　　43

7 Unforced Errors　　47

8 The Bucket - Predictability — 51
8.1 Mixing Strategies in Other Domains — 54

9 Playing in the Wind — 61

10 Variability and Winning — 67

11 Pickleball and Longevity — 73

III PERSONAL STRATEGIES — 77

12 Probability — 79
12.1 Definition of Probability — 79
12.2 Probability in Pickleball — 81

13 Letting the Ball Go — 84

14 The Serve — 90
14.1 Some Practical Results — 97

15 The Third Shot Drop — 99
15.1 Some Practical Results — 103

16 Summary — 107

Part I

INTRODUCTION

CHAPTER 1

Pickleball and the Book

1.1 A Brief History of Pickleball

Pickleball is a young sport that is exploding in popularity.

Although the origins of the game are now well-known and documented, the story is good and worth repeating.

Pickleball was invented in 1965 on Bainbridge Island, Washington, by three friends - Joel Pritchard, Bill Bell, and Barney McCallum. These friends were on summer vacation with their families, and the story goes that their children were bored and were looking for a new game to play. The three men patched together a game using discarded items including a wiffle ball, a badminton net, and some old ping pong paddles. The game was popular with the families, they tinkered with the rules and soon the men began promoting the game more widely.

An old legend has it that the peculiar name "pickleball" was a tribute to Pritchard's dog, who was named Pickles. Although the story is appealing, research involving the original family members reveals that the dog Pickles was born three years later, in 1968. Thus, rather than the game pickleball being named in homage to the dog Pickles, Pickles was named in homage to pickleball. The name pickleball has been attributed to Pritchard's wife Joan. Apparently in the sport of rowing, the leftover and unselected participants from

Chapter 1. Pickleball and the Book

crews formed the "pickle boat". Therefore, just as the pickle boat was formed from a mishmash of rowers, pickleball was formed from a mishmash of household objects.

Whereas each of the inventors was cooperative and had a hand in the development and promotion of pickleball, it might be said that McCallum had the innovative spirit of manufacturing. The first pickleball paddles were made out of plywood in McCallum's home shop. He was also instrumental in the manufacturing of the specialized balls used in pickleball. Pritchard was a businessman and politician who served in the US House of Representatives for the State of Washington, and it was through his domestic travels and events that the game blossomed. Bell too, was instrumental in the development of the sport of pickleball - he expanded and promoted the game, building courts throughout Australia and countries in Southeast Asia.

Pickleball has grown rapidly from its humble beginnings. In 1984, the United States Amateur Pickleball Association (USAPA) was formed with the objective to perpetuate the growth and advancement of pickleball within the United States. The USAPA published the first official pickleball rule book. The USAPA went through various structural changes and adopted the name USA Pickleball (USAP) in 2020. There are now two international pickleball bodies, the International Pickleball Federation (IPF) with over 80 member countries and the World Pickleball Federation (WPF) with over 60 member countries.

Today, pickleball has taken off. According to a 2023 report from the Association of Pickleball Players (APP)[1], pickleball is the fastest growing sport in the U.S. with nearly 50 million Americans having

---
[1] See https://www.theapp.global

played pickleball at least once in the previous year. The report goes on to say that the average age of an avid pickleballer is slightly under 35 years. Participation rates continue to be strong in the over-55 age cohort and across genders. There are now various professional pickleball leagues/tours including Major League Pickleball (MLP) and the Carvana Professional Pickleball Association (PPA) tour.

Some describe pickleball as an amalgam of tennis, badminton and ping pong. The game is played with a hard paddle and a type of wiffle ball. Although pickleball has a singles version of the sport, it is doubles pickleball (i.e. teams of two players) that enjoys the greatest popularity, and is the subject of this book. Pickleball has a particular appeal to seniors as the physical component is less rigorous than in many sports. In Chapter 2, we briefly describe the rules associated with doubles pickleball.

1.2 Evolution in Sport

Given the short history of pickleball, it makes sense that the game of pickleball is actively evolving. Evolution in sport is a natural progression as more people become interested and want to improve. Let me provide two examples of major evolutionary changes in mainstream sports.

In the National Basketball Association (NBA), the three point shot was introduced in the 1979/1980 season. Prior to that, all field goals in basketball were worth two points. With the three point line, successful baskets taken from beyond the line are awarded three points instead of two points. There have been some rule changes with respect to the three point boundary in the NBA over time; however,

Chapter 1. Pickleball and the Book

these changes have been relatively minor[2].

It took a while for teams to realize the scoring potential of the three point shot in the sense that you do not require the same success percentage to generate the same number of points. For example, 4 successful three point shots out of 10 attempts (40% success rate) generates 12 points whereas it takes 6 successful two point shots out of 10 attempts (60% success rate) to generate 12 points.

With this recognition, more three point shots have been attempted over the passage of time, and more training to improve this specialized skill has been emphasized. In summary, more priority is now given to three point shooting.

In Figure 1.1, we plot the average number of three points shots taken per game each season, beginning in the inaugural 1979/1980 season. It is clear that the volume of three point shooting has dramatically increased. There may even be an indication that the number of shots per game has reached a plateaux over the last five years, and perhaps the evolution has stopped, or at least slowed down. We also observe a slight upward bump in attempts during the 1994/1995 through 1996/1997 seasons when the three point line distance was temporarily shortened.

In Figure 1.2, we plot the three point shot success rate over seasons. Here, it is clear that players have improved their three point shooting. There was great improvement from the introduction of the three point line in 1979/1980 until the mid-1990's. Subsequently, the improvement has been less dramatic. Now, the average three point shooter has a success rate exceeding 35%. On offense, there are

---

[2]Initially, the line was 23 feet, 9 inches from the basket to the top of the key, and 22 feet from the basket to the corners. Later in the 1994/1995 season, the line was shortened to 22 feet from the basket in all directions, therefore forming a boundary with a semi-circular shape. The original line was then restored in the 1997/1998 season.

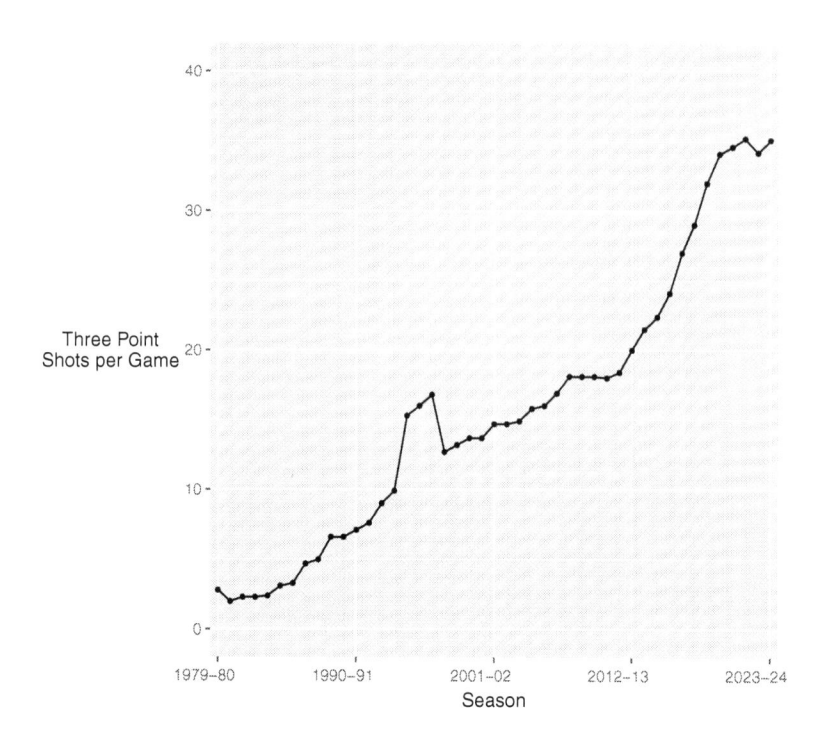

Figure 1.1: Average number of three point attempts per game in the NBA plotted over seasons.

specialists who mostly sit out at the three point line waiting for a pass so that they can take a three point shot. Thus, the NBA game has evolved with respect to three point shooting.

As a second example of evolution in sport, I now discuss the tactic of "pulling the goalie" in the National Hockey League (NHL).

To keep it simple, suppose that a team is losing by exactly one goal in a match, and there are no penalties. In this case, we say that both teams are at full strength which means that the teams are playing 5v5 (ie. five skaters versus five skaters) where we do not count the goaltenders. Late in the game, it has become standard practice for the trailing team to replace their goaltender with a regular skater. In this case, the trailing team is now playing 6v5 which provides a

Chapter 1. Pickleball and the Book 7

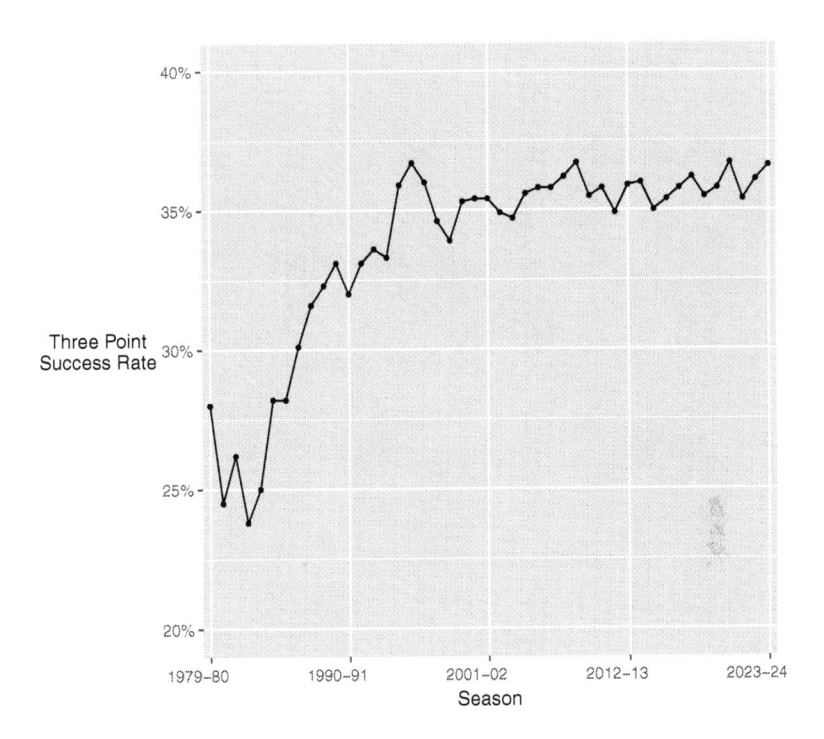

Figure 1.2: Three point shot success percentage plotted over seasons.

manpower advantage and increases the trailing team's probability of scoring a tying goal. On the other hand, since the trailing team's goaltender has been *pulled*, and their net is empty, the leading team is also more likely to score and increase their lead by two goals.

Given the risks that face the trailing team that pulls their goalie, the key question is when, exactly, should they do it? For a long time in the NHL, pulling the goalie took place with roughly one minute remaining in the match.

The one-minute tactic was essentially a tradition. It had not been tested using data or assessed with quantitative rigor. I think a reason for this is that players are often coached by former players, who were coached by former players, etc. Hence, traditions (which may be myths) often have wide acceptance and take a long time to undergo scrutiny.

However, with respect to pulling the goalie, there was some work done in the sports analytics literature, via the study of goal scoring rates and the use of simulations. The investigations suggested that pulling the goalie with more than one minute remaining might be a better strategy. One such publication[3] suggested that the trailing team ought to pull their goalie with approximately three minutes remaining in the game.

The above advice was counterintuitive to many hockey people, including coaches. Pulling the goalie so early almost ensured that a goal would be scored, and the goal would more likely be scored against the trailing team with the empty net. But this sentiment misses the point; the trailing team is losing and it does not really matter if they lose by one goal or two goals. The objective is to try to improve the probability of overcoming the one goal deficit.

It is unclear whether the advice in the journal publication was heeded. However, a trend began where teams trailing by one goal started pulling their goalie earlier than in the past. This trend may have been initiated by coach and former NHL goaltender Patrick Roy. Roy began pulling his goalie earlier than one minute remaining while he was coaching the Quebec Remparts of the Quebec Major Junior Hockey League (QMJHL). Roy continued this seemingly risky approach when he was appointed as head coach of the Colorado Avalanche of the NHL in 2013.

In Figure 1.3, we present the average time to pull the goaltender in the NHL when a team is trailing by exactly one goal. These times are plotted by year over the seasons 2007/2008 through 2020/2021.

---

[3]Beaudoin, D. and Swartz, T.B. (2010). Strategies for pulling the goalie in hockey. The American Statistician, 64(3), 197-204.

Chapter 1. Pickleball and the Book

Over the seasons, we observe an increase in the time remaining to pull the goalie. The time increase has been significant; roughly one and a half minutes. Like the basketball example, this is another example of how strategies evolve slowly in sport. However, this isn't always the case. Sometimes, changes occur suddenly - take the Fosbury Flop, for example. The Fosbury Flop is a high jump technique that was introduced by Dick Fosbury in the 1968 Summer Olympics. Almost immediately, the Fosbury Flop became the standard approach for the high jump.

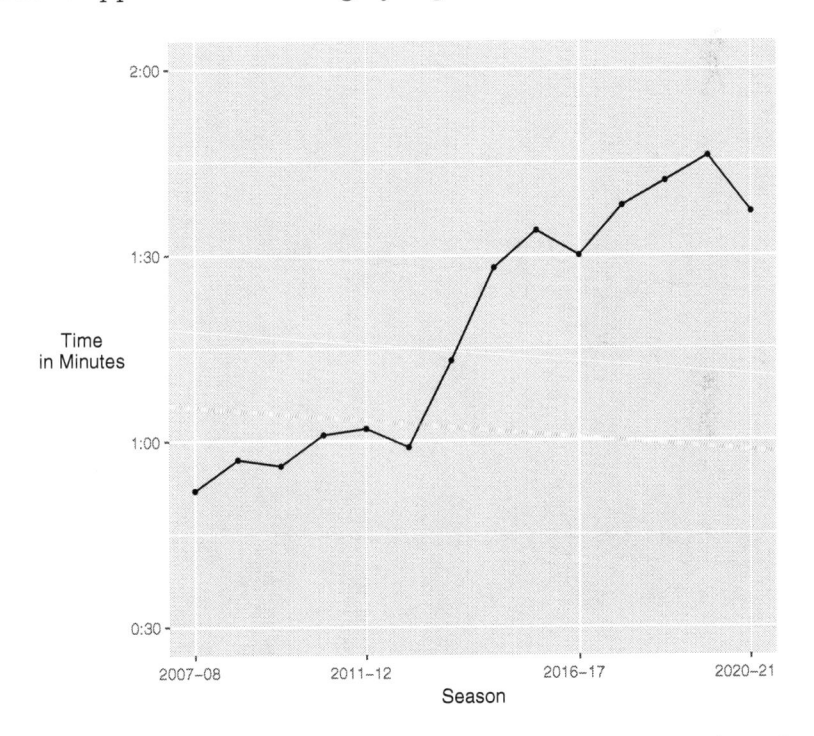

Figure 1.3: Average minutes remaining to pull the goalie when a team is losing by exactly one goal and both teams are at even strength. The times are plotted over seasons.

Since the sport of pickleball is relatively young, it might be expected that pickleball will experience its own evolution. For example, we are already seeing the development and proliferation of expensive paddles made from high tech materials. Some of the new paddles facilitate more spin and produce shots of greater speeds. It is also evident to me that younger people who are flooding to the sport of pickleball play somewhat differently than the older crowd. It is the hope that some of the ideas in this book may be evolutionary, at least on a personal level for you.

1.3 Motivation

Prior to writing this book, I scoured the pickleball literature and instructional videos to understand the current state of strategies and guidance related to doubles pickleball. There is a lot of really good material out there which can help improve your game. For example, you can learn how to warm up properly, how to serve more effectively, have an effective mindset, and many more disparate topics.

But this book is different. This book is not comprehensive in any sense. Rather, I have cherry-picked topics in pickleball that I think are interesting. Therefore, although I call it a book, it is really more of a monograph on topics that interest me. Specifically, I want to present topics of strategy, topics that to my knowledge have not been widely explored or perhaps discussed from a different point of view.

Since a lot of people have been attracted to pickleball, there has been considerable thought about how the game ought to be played. And much of this advice strikes me as solid. Consequently, this book is not long; I am only discussing topics where I think people should give the prevailing wisdom a second look. Since I am swimming upstream on some issues, I ask you to read critically, and ask yourself whether some of the advice applies to you.

Chapter 1. Pickleball and the Book

I approach this book as a Professor of Statistics who has been doing research for more than 40 years. My early research days concerned mainly technical topics such as Bayesian methods. However, sport has always been my passion. And I worked quietly in sports research as a hobby for a long time. However, things began to change in 2003, when Michael Lewis wrote the book "Moneyball", which was followed by the blockbuster movie starring Brad Pitt in 2011. Moneyball concerned the activities of manager Billy Beane of the Oakland A's in Major League Baseball (MLB). Oakland was a small-market MLB team, and through an analytics approach, Beane discovered ways to improve team success in baseball. In a nutshell, analytics is the use of quantitative methods and data to obtain new insights.

Moneyball brought analytics to the consciousness of the general public, and with the advent of more data, sports analytics has become a trendy research topic. Most major professional sports teams now hire analytics staff, and there has been no stopping the movement. With a head start in sports analytics, my research activities in the field took off. On my website[4], you can review some of my activities where I have written on many sports and sports-related topics including American football, basketball, soccer, baseball, hockey, cricket, golf, tennis, rugby, pickleball, bowling, highland dance, gambling, training and drafting.

The analytics perspectives offered in this book provide some novel insights and may help improve your game. The chapters are independent of one another in the sense that if you are uninterested in a particular chapter, you can skip it and it will not affect your reading of the other chapters.

---

[4]See https://www.sfu.ca/~tswartz/

The book is divided into three parts. Part I is introductory and provides some general remarks about pickleball. I especially hope that Chapter 3 "The Pillars of Pickleball" catches your attention. I think it is easy reading.

In Part II, I examine topics in pickleball that you have probably considered. Some of these topics arise from "truths" that were told to me in my early days of pickleball. As a statistician by training, I think I have a cautious nature, and some of these truths did not sit easily with me. I have examined these topics using logical principles including probability theory and game theory. Therefore, I have put forth opinions and musings that may challenge aspects of conventional wisdom. You may find some of this interesting, and I would be happy to hear from you if you have a different point of view on a topic[5]. I am excited to hear about new ideas and perspectives.

Part III is the most novel contribution in the book. I have not seen anyone explore issues in pickleball using the methods proposed here. I use elementary probability theory to help readers assess their personal strategies. Admittedly, this requires the reader to dig in a bit, where I introduce technicalities that are typically presented in a first course in Probability and Statistics. However, I introduce the technical materials from square one, and with some persistence, I believe the content is accessible to a wide audience. If you can gain an appreciation for the technical parts (e.g. assigning your own personal probabilities), then this will assist you in determining optimal personal strategies. You can do this for the examples provided in Chapters 13-15 or in other pickleball contexts. As a by-product, this material may help you identify aspects of your pickleball game that need improvement. And you may inadvertently pick up some

---

[5]You can contact me at tswartz@sfu.ca

Chapter 1. Pickleball and the Book

probabilistic reasoning along the way.

So, for whom is the book written? Of course, it is written for pickleball players. But there is a bit more to it than that. When I began writing, I was thinking that the messaging would be most relevant to mid-level players, say those with a pickleball rating between 3.0 and 4.5. The really top players (ratings 5.0 and above) do play differently than the rest of us. However, a problem with the (3.0-4.5) categorization is that it is not precise. Sometimes, a player with a 3.0 rating at one club might be classified as a 4.0 player at another club. Another problem is that mid-level players possess a diverse set of abilities. Some are more or less strategic, some are more or less athletic, and some are more or less skilled. My optimistic view is that no matter how you play, there should be something in this book for you.

But more important than ability, this book is directed to pickleball players who like to look at issues with a critical lens and who want to think carefully about their personal strategies. The book will require some careful reading in parts, especially in Part III. But I hope at the end of the day, you can reflect on some of the topics and apply them to your game.

Happy pickling!

Chapter 2

The Rules of Pickleball

This short chapter may be omitted by those who are familiar with doubles pickleball. In this chapter, I am going to describe the basic rules and some terminology. I will not discuss technical details such as what makes a serve legal. For the complete rules, one may download the Global Pickleball Federation Official Rulebook[1]. Despite the general simplicity of pickleball, the 2024 Official Rulebook is 76 pages long.

The pickleball court is depicted in Figure 2.1. The court is 44 feet long, divided in the middle by a net. The net is 3 feet tall at the ends, but a little shorter (34 inches) in the middle. Extending from the net on both sides is the 7-foot non-volley zone (NVZ) which will be discussed later. The non-volley zone is commonly referred to as the *kitchen*. The court is 20 feet wide. A pickleball court is a little less than half the size (area) of a tennis court.

A pickleball match is won when a team reaches 11 points. However, a team must win by at least two points, and therefore, matches can be extended to scores such as 15-13. Teams can only score points when they are serving. If your team loses 11-0, then it is said that your team has been *pickled*.

A determination is made (sometimes using a coin flip) as to which team initiates serving. In Figure 2.1, we use the symbols S and R to

---

[1]See https://globalpickleballfederation.org/pickleball-rulebook/

Chapter 2. The Rules of Pickleball   15

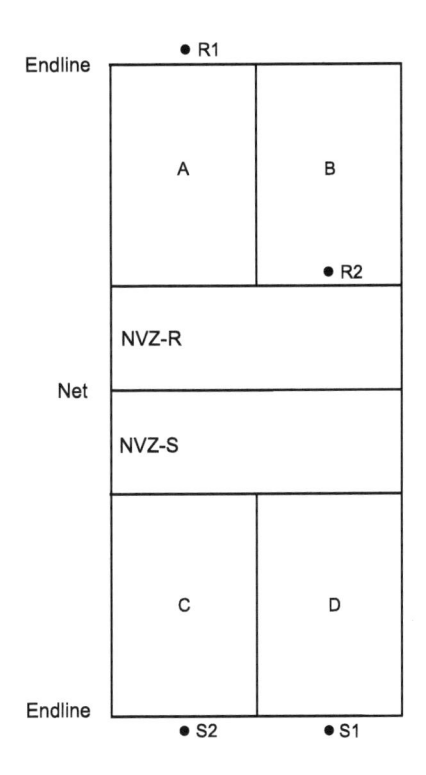

Figure 2.1: The pickleball court with regions of interest A, B, C and D. The depicted setup has S1 serving to R1. S2 (the partner of S1) and R2 (the partner of R1) are shown in their typical starting positions.

denote the serving team and the receiving team, respectively. Service then alternates between the two teams. There is a notion of first and second serves, and it may seem peculiar that the team that initiates serving begins with their second serves. In other words, the team serving at the beginning of the match is only allotted their second serves. From this point of the match forward, as service alternates, each team is allotted both their first and second serves.

Expanding on the service protocol, suppose that it is the beginning of a match. It is then the second serve, and the player marked S1 in Figure 2.1 begins serving. S1 must stand on the right hand side of the court (sometimes call the *even court*), and must stand behind the endline. Typically, the partner S2 initially stands as shown in Figure 2.1 although this is not required by the rules. And typically, the receiving team members R1 and R2 stand as shown in Figure 2.1 to receive the serve, although again, this is not required by the rules. S1 attempts to make an underhand serve that lands somewhere in region A. Now, if the S1/S2 team wins the rally (more on that later), they receive a point, S1 and S2 change their initial serving positions, and S1 attempts to make another second serve (this time from the *odd court*) that lands somewhere in region B. As long as S1 and S2 win rallies, they continue to accumulate points, S1 and S2 continue to alternate positions and S1 continues to make second serves. However, the moment that S1 and S2 lose a rally, then no points are scored, and service reverts to the opponents R1 and R2. This is called a *side out*.

With the change of service, R1 begins with their first serve from their even court. As R1 and R2 (now the serving team) win rallies, they accumulate points, they change positions and R1 makes another first serve. However, once R1 and R2 lose a rally, then no points are scored, and it becomes second serve where R2 is the server beginning in the court where R2 was located when the previous rally was lost. The same procedure then continues with R2 as the second server until R1 and R2 lose a rally. Service then reverts back (side out) to the opponents S1 and S2 where they begin their first serves.

Now that the point scoring procedure and the serving rotation have been established, we need to describe how a rally is won. As described, there is a symmetry regarding the positioning of the two

Chapter 2. The Rules of Pickleball

teams and the even/odd sides of the court. Therefore, we will only describe the situation where S1 is serving from the even court as depicted in Figure 2.1. As a rally progresses, there are slightly different rules regarding the first shot, the second shot, the third shot, and subsequent shots. From the fourth shot onward, the rules are the same. Let's discuss the rules surrounding each of these shots. It is more convenient to describe the situations that would cause the team hitting the shot to lose the rally. Note that a *volley* refers to a shot that is hit in the air before it bounces on the court.

Consider the first shot (i.e. the serve) by S1. Then S1 and S2 lose the rally if any of the following occur:

- the serve hits the net
- the serve lands outside of region A

Subsequently, consider the second shot by the R1/R2 team following a legitimate first shot (i.e. serve). R1 and R2 lose the rally if any of the following occur:

- the ball bounces twice or they fail to make contact
- the returned shot is volleyed
- the returned shot hits the net
- the returned shot lands outside (NVZ-S, C, D)

Subsequently, consider the third shot by the S1/S2 team following a legitimate second shot. S1 and S2 lose the rally if any of the following occur:

- the ball bounces twice or they fail to make contact
- the returned shot is volleyed
- the returned shot hits the net
- the returned shot lands outside (NVZ-R, A, B)

Subsequently, consider the fourth shot by the R1/R2 team following a legitimate third shot. R1 and R2 lose the rally if any of the following occur:

- the ball bounces twice or they fail to make contact
- the returned shot is volleyed from within NVZ-R
- the returned shot hits the net
- the returned shot lands outside (NVZ-S, C, D)

Although it is easy for a beginner to pick up the rules of doubles pickleball by playing for a short period of time, writing the rules concisely and digesting them is a little more challenging. The above description of the rules is as succinct as I have seen.

CHAPTER 3

The Pillars of Pickleball

The sport of pickleball is taking off. The popularity may partly be due to the unique culture of the game. For example, there is a social element to the sport, and there is an ethos of helping your competitors. Matches are reasonably short in pickleball (typically 15 minutes), and therefore, playing pickleball does not require a huge commitment; this seems attractive compared to a sport like test cricket where matches can take up to five days and not produce a winner.

In addition, the barriers to the sport are relatively modest. The rules are fairly simple and the key action of hitting the ball over the net is easily learned. About the only things you need for doubles pickleball are a paddle, a ball, three buddies and access to a court.

There is also an aspect of inclusivity in the sport that many people find appealing. In how many sports can you find men competing against women, and 70-year olds competing favorably against 20-somethings? There have been many times when I have looked at someone, anticipated their level based on their appearance, and have been completely wrong. I think that the potential to compete broadly is a key feature as to why people enjoy pickleball.

This brings up the question: what are the winning components in pickleball? It seems to me that the necessary ingredients of success in pickleball are skill, athleticism, strategy and luck. I want to discuss each of these elements in turn, but what I think is really interesting is that none of these ingredients is dominant. In other words, your team may be superior to the opposition in any one of the four ingredients, but that may not be enough to win the match.

3.1 Skill

No doubt, skill forms a major component of success in pickleball.

What is skill? According to a dictionary source, it is the ability to do something well. In some sports, particular skills are unachievable for many of us. For example, in the sport of basketball, I am never going to be able to "dunk" a basketball. Similarly, in soccer, a bicycle kick[1] is now out of the question for me. In pickleball, I think that most skills are achievable. It is the precise execution of the skill and the rate at which you can carry it out that determines your skill level. For example, someone who is successful hitting the third shot drop 70% of the time has a higher skill level than someone who is successful hitting the third shot drop only 50% of the time. By precise execution, I mean, for example, that a third shot drop landing in the non-volley zone is more precise than a third shot dropping landing just outside the non-volley zone. The third shot drop is discussed more fully in Chapter 15.

The good news about skill is that there is something that you can do about it - practice. Although most players would like to improve, many do not practice frequently. They simply play and hope to get better. Think about your serve for a moment. If you play a match, you may only serve about 10 times in the game. However, if you

---

[1] A bicycle kick is executed by somersaulting backwards and kicking the ball in midair as if in a pedaling motion.

Chapter 3. The Pillars of Pickleball   21

go out with a friend (who collects balls and does not even need to know the game), with multiple balls at your disposal, you can easily practice 100 serves over 15 minutes. This is roughly the same time that it takes to play a match.

Moreover, when you practice the same task in succession, you can readily observe the impact of small modifications (e.g. adding a little more spin to your serve). In addition, attempting a wild and risky idea is something that you may entertain during practice but are unwilling to implement in a game until you have developed confidence in the approach.

Technique is also related to skill. There may be various ways of implementing a skill. Having good technique helps you to perform the skill at a high level. For example, your grip on the paddle may effect your control which in turn impacts your skill to hit a dink shot. There is a lot of advice in the pickleball universe concerning good technique.

Let's conclude this short section by producing a non-exhaustive list of pickleball skills: the serve, the drop shot, the dink shot, the offensive lob, the defensive lob, volleys, topspin shots, undersrpin shots, sidespin shots, the overhead smash shot, the block shot, backhand shots, the ernie, positioning, footwork, etc. Again, there is lots of information out there related to each of these skills.

3.2 Athleticism

There is not really much to say about athleticism. With all things being equal, athleticism confers an advantage.

Athleticism manifests itself in various ways in the sport of pickleball. It includes moving quicker (speed), and reacting faster (acceleration). Note that speed and acceleration are not the same thing, and that the importance of acceleration is gaining wider recognition in sport[2]. Being physically fit is also useful, especially during long hot days on the pickleball court. It is well known that cognitive responses required in sport deteriorate as one tires. Body control and flexibility also have a role in pickleball. They impact your ability to maneuver, reach balls and return shots. What about strength? You might argue that hitting the ball hard is easier for the stronger player. However, some might say that this is more of a function of technique. Although being tall and having a long wingspan is not really an athletic feature, it is part of your personal makeup and it is clearly an advantage in pickleball.

There are clearly limits on the degree that you can improve your athleticism. Lots of training does not make you much faster, for example. There are also practical constraints (e.g. time) that may prevent you from the training required to improve your athleticism. And, of course, athleticism is fleeting. Father time is undefeated in sport. Even though pickleball is very popular amongst seniors, you do not see many seniors playing professional pickleball. Various rankings suggest that Ben Johns may be the best pickleball player in the world (2025). At the time of writing, Ben Johns is only 25 years old.

3.3 Strategy

There are many specific strategies in pickleball. For example, it is usually better to hit the ball towards a player's backhand than

---

[2]Guan, T. and Swartz, T.B. (2024). Acceleration and age in sport. International Journal of Sports Science and Coaching, 19(3), 1035-1041.

Chapter 3. The Pillars of Pickleball

to their forehand since their forehand shot is typically stronger and more reliable. It is also usually better to hit more shots to the weaker opponent in doubles pickleball. These strategies are well known and are discussed in length in many books and videos. However, there is a simplified description as to how the game ought to be played. We conveniently refer to the serving team by S (to denote serving) and the returning team by R (to denote returning). Most avid pickleballers would agree that strategic doubles pickleball typically proceeds as follows:

1. S hits a deep serve (i.e. near the endline)

2. R hits a deep return and approaches the non-volley zone

3. S hits a third shot drop and approaches the non-volley zone

4. R and S engage in *dinking* (i.e. soft shots near the net)

5. A team becomes aggressive, and the game is sped up

6. A team wins the rally or a soft shot reverts the rally to step 4

The above steps provide a baseline for standard pickleball strategy. Of course, there are caveats to these strategies. The caveats depend on issues such as avoiding predictability (see Chapter 8) and assessing player success rates in executing particular shots (see Part III of the book).

Ideally, the above steps should be ingrained in muscle memory. These are the steps that you do without thinking. Playing well is difficult; to simultaneously play and make active decisions is most challenging. You would like your game to reach a level where your baseline reactions are strategically sound. That is, you play enough and you think about your game enough (off the court) that you instinctively make solid choices most of the time. The best time to strategize is before a match. If you are familiar with your partner and your opponents, perhaps you can make slight adjustments that will help things go more your way.

During a match, there is not usually enough time to transition between strategies. In some competitions, time-outs are available to speak to your partner. Adjustments at this point would require recognition of what is taking place and some quick thinking on your part. For example, maybe you recognize that one of your opponents is *poaching* (i.e. moving over and playing shots that the other opponent would typically play). If you observe this, then it might be recommended to play more of your shots to the space that the poacher is vacating. As a second example, suppose while serving, you observe that your right handed opponent shades far to their left side so that they can return serves with their stronger right forehand. In this case, it may be strategic to hit your serves farther to the opponent's right hand side to make them chase the serve.

Also, sometimes we do not tend to see things as they really are when they pertain to us. If you have pickleball friends, seek their advice regarding strategic aspects of your game.

3.4 Luck

An often overlooked aspect of pickleball success is luck. In some sports, the best team wins most of the time, and this is often due to a probabilistic phenomenon known as the *law of large numbers*. For example, a basketball match is a long slog; each team has possession of the ball roughly 100 times during a game. Therefore, even though the weaker team may have success on some possessions, over the

Chapter 3. The Pillars of Pickleball

long haul, the better team usually reveals itself and typically wins the game.

This is contrasted with pickleball where the first team to score 11 points wins the match. Achieving 11 points is only a moderate hurdle, and therefore, it does not take a lot of unusual events to sway the outcome of a match. For example, suppose the ball hits the net and drops over a couple of times in one team's favor during a match. This happens now and then. Also, frequently there are "gimme" shots that players typically make that are blown. These unexpected events can impact the outcomes of matches (see the related discussion of unforced errors in Chapter 7). I am sure that you have personal experiences in pickleball where weaker teams have won matches against stronger teams.

Well, maybe you would argue that when a weaker team defeats a stronger team in pickleball that this is not a case of luck, but rather that the weaker team played better. Fair enough. However, what I am really trying to say is that there is less predictability in short duration sports such as pickleball. To investigate this, I coded a pickleball simulator with pickleball games terminating at the standard 11 points, and also pickleball games terminating at a hypothetical 21 points. For illustration, I set the weaker pickleball team winning 45% of the rallys with the stronger team winning 55% of the rallys. This is not completely realistic but it is useful for demonstration purposes. In the 11-point matches, the weaker team wins 25% of the games, and in the 21-point matches, the weaker team wins only 18% of the games. If these results seems a bit puzzling, think about an absurd competition where a match terminates at one million points. Here, the stronger team (by virtue of winning 55% of the rallies) always wins. The point again is that in short matches such as pickleball, almost anybody can win if they get a bit lucky.

If there is a practical lesson related to luck, it may be to not give up in pickleball. Because 11 winning points is not a huge threshold, weaker teams can defeat stronger teams and deficits can be overcome. Keep plugging.

Part II

MUSINGS ON STRATEGY

There is a lot of pickleball advice out there. I think this is partly due to the fervor associated with this modern game. It also has something to do with the pickleball personality which strikes me as generous. Many players really do want to help one another.

However, how does advice/strategy reach a consensus? Is it the case (such as in politics) that if people say something often enough, it becomes accepted as the truth?

There has been advice/strategy that has come my way that has caused me to think twice about it. In Chapters 4-11, I explore some topics of advice/strategy from a different perspective. I have used various tools of analytics in the exploration. Although you may find some of it counterintuitive, I hope you will find it interesting.

CHAPTER 4

Parking the Bus

Have you heard of José Mourinho? He is a famous soccer manager. Mourinho has a long and impressive record, having won 26 senior trophies while coaching major soccer clubs across Europe and in England. In particular, he has won the Champions League[1] competition twice, while manager at FC Porto and also at Inter Milan.

Mourinho, also self-described as "the Special One", gives colorful interviews and is often quoted. For example, describing his lack of confidence in young players, he once said, "Young players are like melons. Only when you open and taste the melon, are you 100% sure that the melon is good." Another expression attributed to Mourinho is the negatively perceived term "parking the bus" where he refers to a playing style in soccer that is extremely defensive and is widely viewed as boring. When a soccer team parks the bus, it is as though a bus is blocking their defensive goal, where the players maintain a compact shape, and the team demonstrates minimal ambition going forward in attack. The team's sole intention is to prevent the opponent from scoring. Parking the bus is a strategy that is often used when a team is leading and is attempting to protect the lead.

---

[1]The Champions League is the world's greatest soccer club competition held annually by the Union of European Football Associations (UEFA) and is contested by top-European clubs who qualify for participation.

Chapter 4. Parking the Bus

The strategy of protecting a lead by playing defensively is pervasive across sports. For example, I have witnessed the strategy in American football, basketball and hockey. In basketball, you may see a leading team using up the shot clock late in the game to reduce the remaining number of possessions, and consequently, reduce the number of scoring opportunities for the opponent. With fewer opportunities, the thought is that the leading team ought to be better able to protect the lead.

As a consequence, sporting people have wondered whether playing extremely defensively is a solid strategy. In particular, people have posited that it is a poor strategy. For example, in the National Football League (NFL), former coach John Madden once stated, "All a prevent defense does is prevent you from winning". In a prevent defense, the team that is leading and is playing defence, allows the opponent to make small gains, while limiting long plays down the field that could more quickly result in scoring. However, the small gains often add up and defeat the purpose of protecting the lead.

The difficulty with assessing the strategy of parking the bus in soccer is that a team's defensive strategy is confounded with the opponent's offensive strategy. In other words, is Team A playing extremely defensively or is it the case that team B is playing extremely offensively? Or is a combination of both approaches? However, a recent journal article[2] disentangled a team's defensive ambitions from the opponent's offensive ambitions in soccer, and concluded that parking the bus is not a beneficial strategy.

This line of research has caused me to consider widely accepted defensive strategies in pickleball. Perhaps some of the advice about

---

[2] Guan, T., Cao, J. and Swartz, T.B. (2023). Parking the bus. Journal of Quantitative Analysis in Sports, 19(4), 263-272.

Chapter 4. Parking the Bus

"not making mistakes in pickleball" ought to be reconsidered. A mistake in pickleball is an action which nearly immediately leads to a lost rally. The unwillingness to risk making mistakes in pickleball is analogous to playing extremely defensively or parking the bus.

Moreover, I believe that there is a pickleball culture where mid-level players tend to play on the cautious side. And by cautious, I mean overcautious. I suspect that some players are more concerned about losing rallies due to mistakes than by winning rallies due to good play.

Maybe, some pickleball players take the advice to be cautious too seriously, and as a result, they are not sufficiently aggressive. In all walks of life, including pickleball, there are sometimes benefits in taking risks.

So, how do we address this problem? How do you know whether you are playing too defensively or too aggressively in pickleball? The answer is that it depends. It depends on the ability of players to successfully execute particular shots. Therefore, whether you should play more defensively or more aggressively is a personal decision. I suggest that the way to make these assessments is through investigations via probability as outlined in Part III of the book.

4.1 Cautious Play in Pickleball

Let's put probabilistic investigations to the side for the moment. Instead, I wish to discuss five general strategies which may cause some people to play too defensively. I think there are more situations than these in pickleball regarding the defensive/aggressive dilemma, but let's stick with these cases. After I list the five strategies, I will discuss each strategy in turn from a qualitative point of view.

Chapter 4. Parking the Bus

Here are five common pickleball strategies that definitely lie on the cautious side of the spectrum:

(i) Never hit your serve into the net nor out of bounds

(ii) Keep dinking, and let your opponent make the mistake

(iii) Don't aim "down the lines" as you may hit the ball out

(iv) Don't lob since it is difficult to control

(v) Don't creep up from the endline prior to the third shot

Strategy (i): It has been stated by some top pickleball coaches[3] that you should not "miss your serve more than once per month". Perhaps this is hyperbole with the real intent being "don't miss your serve often". However, if I were to miss my serve only once per month, with roughly 10 serves per match, 8 matches per day and 12 playing days per month, this would mean that I could only miss a serve about 0.1% of the time (i.e., about one time out of a thousand serves). Clearly, this is impossible for me.

If I attempted to miss my serve only 0.1% of the time, I would need to execute an extremely cautious serve, one that is in the middle, not hit hard and not hit with much spin. I would need to hit my serve so meekly, that even if I made a slight mishit, the ball would still land in play. The consequence of such a serve is that my opponent would find my serve incredibly easy to handle.

And if my serve is easy to handle, this provides an advantage to the other team in at least two ways: (1) they will be able to approach the non-volley zone quickly and easily, and (2) they will

---
[3] See page 197 in Movsessian, R. and Baker, J. (2018). How to Play Pickleball: The Complete Guide from A to Z. ISBN-13: 978-1-7239-9308-4.

Chapter 4. Parking the Bus

have an opportunity to hit a good second shot that causes difficulty for me. Consequently, playing it safe gives my opponents the upper hand. Perhaps I will have more overall success if my serve poses some level of challenge to my opponent, even if it hits the net or goes out of bounds occasionally? In Chapter 14, we investigate the probabilistic aspects of strategy related to the serve.

Strategy (ii): I have sometimes heard the sentiment that once a rally reaches the "short game" with both teams dinking, you should exercise patience, hang in there, continue dinking, and wait for the opponent to make a mistake.

This sounds plausible, but what if the opponent is better at dinking than you? Then you are the one who is more likely to make the first mistake (e.g. hit the ball into the net or pop the ball up). In this case, should you still be patient?

And what does it really mean to make a mistake? When the opponent pops the ball up where you can smash it, everyone would agree that the pop-up is a mistake. The net is 36 inches (3 feet) tall at the sidelines, and 34 inches tall in the middle. Therefore, a 5-foot pop-up is definitely a mistake. But is a 4-foot pop-up a mistake? Introducing topspin, you may be able to return that 4-foot pop-up effectively and with pace. I am saying that the notion of a defining a mistake in the dinking phase is not black and white - there is a gray area where the decision between going from defense (continue dinking) versus attacking is not straightforward. The decision depends on your ability, your opponent's ability and the surprise element. If you rarely go on offense from the dinking phase, you may be playing too cautiously.

Strategy (iii): Pickleball players are rarely encouraged to hit the ball down the lines. Hitting the ball down the sidelines is often said to be risky because you may end up hitting the ball wide and out of bounds. Instead, I often hear the mantra that you should try to hit the ball between the two opponents ("down the middle"). Down the middle is surely good advice if there is a sufficient space between the two players and you have a good opportunity of hitting the ball to a spot that neither player can reach.

But in terms of outcome, hitting a ball down the sidelines and in bounds that the opponents cannot reach is no different than hitting the ball down the middle that the opponents cannot reach. Both are great shots.

The real issue here is execution. How frequently can you hit the ball down the sidelines and in bounds that your opponents cannot reach? And how frequently can you hit the ball down the middle that your opponents cannot reach? The answer to this depends on the width of the gap where you are aiming, and again, your skill level and the skill level of your opponents. You may be playing too cautiously if you rarely hit a ball down the sidelines.

Strategy (iv): There is a recommendation that you should not hit lob shots. There are two types of lob shots in pickleball. A defensive lob occurs when you are in trouble. Maybe you are in no man's land (i.e. somewhere between the non-volley zone and the endline) and your opponents are pounding the ball at you. You attempt to get some relief by hitting the ball over their heads and making them back up. The defensive lob also provides some additional time for you to move to a more solid defensive position. An offensive lob typically occurs when both teams have approached the non-volley zone, and you attempt to win the rally by flipping the ball over your opponent's head, perhaps with not such as high an arc as with the defensive lob.

Chapter 4. Parking the Bus

Lob shots are risky for two reasons: (1) you may hit a short lob, giving your opponent the opportunity to smash the ball, and (2) you may hit a long lob which is out of bounds. You need to hit the lob shot close to perfect, which would bounce (if left untouched) near the endline. When comparing pickleball to tennis, the tennis court is deeper which makes it easier to keep the tennis lob from going out of bounds beyond the endline.

So, should pickleballers stop hitting lob shots since they are risky? One response is that instead of eliminating lobs from your pickleball toolkit, you should just improve your lob shot so that it more frequently travels the proper distance (neither too short nor too long). Then, there are similar retorts to those used with the previously discussed strategies. For example, the surprise element of the lob can be beneficial. Also, you have to weigh the value of winning a rally via a successful lob versus the downside of an unsuccessful lob. This topic can be investigated using the approach described in Part III.

Personally, I like the offensive lob more than the defensive lob since the offensive lob can immediately result in winning a rally. With a defensive lob, more things have to go right for you following the lob, before you win the rally. Also, I think that a drop shot (although possibly difficult to execute under the circumstances of a defensive lob) is often a better alternative than a defensive lob. In the risk/reward ratio, the offensive lob has both lesser risk (i.e. fewer bad things can happen) and greater reward (i.e. more good things can happen) than the defensive lob.

Strategy (v): I have been lectured by various pickleball partners when I have "crept up" following our serve. That is, I have moved forward from the endline too early. The alternative to creeping is to

Chapter 4. Parking the Bus

stay behind the endline and wait for the second shot to develop.

The logic of the widely accepted no-creeping strategy follows from the rule that the serving team cannot volley the third shot. If you creep and the returning team hits the ball near the endline on the second shot, you may have to step back and let the ball bounce. The backward step entails hitting a more difficult third shot. So again, this is caution imposing itself - don't creep because something bad may happen.

My question is how often can the returning team hit the wonder second shot that lands one foot from the endline and causes you to back up? My experience as a mid-level player is that they cannot do it frequently. It is too risky for them - they may hit the ball out of bounds and immediately lose the rally. The benefit of creeping on the third shot is that you can get to the non-volley zone quicker and with momentum. You may also benefit by reaching a short second shot quicker. Consequently, you may hit a better third shot. For many players, it is not such a big deal to take a step back if the returning team hits a great second shot. I see various benefits of creeping; creeping has little risk and considerable reward.

In summary, the five examples have illustrated that there is a lot of pickleball advice that is of a cautious nature. In Chapter 1, I spoke about evolution in sport. Perhaps pickleball will evolve with a greater emphasis on attempting to win rallies rather than trying to avoid losing rallies. In other words, maybe pickleballers will move away from parking the bus. At the very least, I hope that you are willing to entertain the idea that playing too cautiously may sometimes be a negative strategy. Finally, if you are going to try to be less cautious and attempt more aggressive options, you ought to be able to do these things well.

Chapter 5

Approaching the Net

In pickleball, there are various strategic principles that are associated with winning. However, most strategies should not be adhered to *all of the time*. There are at least two reasons for this opinion. First, you should not allow yourself to become predictable (see Chapter 8). If your opponent knows what you are about to do, this is an obvious disadvantage. The second reason for not adhering to a strategic principle is that there may be contexts where the principle is not optimal. Here, I illustrate the second reason using an example that concerns team alignment. The example is examined using geometrical considerations.

The widely accepted strategic principle that I would like to explore is that teammates ought to approach the net together, up to the non-volley zone (NVZ), and that they are symbolically tied together by an invisible but rigid string. This advice has also been described as "staying in line with your partner".

Most of the time, approaching the NVZ together with your partner is a good principle. Doing so tends to reduce the size of gaps where your opponents may hit the ball. However, there may be contexts where it is not ideal. We now illustrate such a context.

For example, imagine the following situation. Your team is in a good advanced position, having reached the NVZ. However, at this stage, your team pops the ball up, and you anticipate that your

Chapter 5. Approaching the Net

opponent is about to hit a hard volley back at you. Your team is now in a vulnerable position.

The position of your opponent who is about to volley the ball is depicted with an X in Figure 5.1. A key aspect of the scenario is that you know that player X is going to hit the ball hard; maybe this player is very predictable. For illustration, the opponent X is positioned 2.5 feet from the sideline and 4.0 feet back from the NVZ. In this figure, you and your partner are positioned according to the general principle that you have advanced together and have reached the "ideal" location, at the edge of the NVZ. I have made a few small assumptions. For example, assume that you and your partner are 8.0 feet apart from one another and you each have wingspans of 7.0 feet. That is, you can extend your reach to the ball both 3.5 feet to the left and 3.5 feet to the right. With such a wingspan and the 8.0 foot spacing between you and your partner, there is a gap of 1.0 foot between you and your partner that cannot be reached. The seemingly longish wingspan takes into account the extension of the paddle.

In Figure 5.1, the defensive gaps (i.e. the locations that your team cannot reach) are illustrated by regions A, B, and C. These are the locations where the opponent may consider aiming. For example, region A is a rectangular gap that is 2.5 feet wide and stretches down the left sideline. So, where is your opponent about to hit the hard volley? Your opponent is reluctant to aim for regions A and C since these regions border the sidelines, and the ball may easily go out of bounds. Therefore, we focus on region B ("down the middle") where the opponent is most likely to aim. Have a close look at region B. The regions have been drawn to scale taking into account pickleball court dimensions.

Chapter 5. Approaching the Net

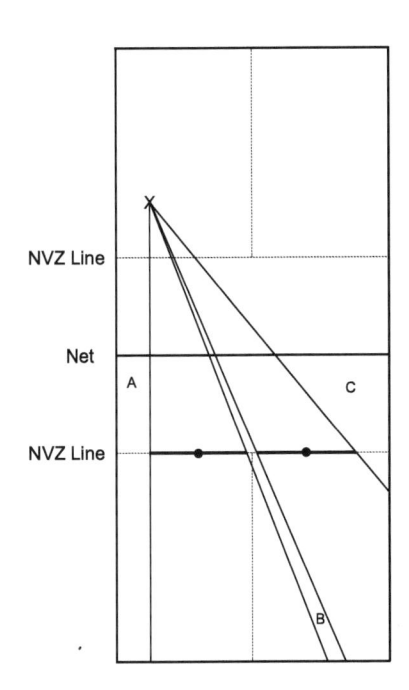

Figure 5.1: Gap regions A, B and C based on standard positioning. The symbol X denotes your opponent executing the volley and the two dots represent you and your partner who are attempting to return the shot. You and your partner are positioned at the edge of the non-volley zone with your team's total wingspan depicted by the bolded line.

Let's pause for a second. You may object that the two dots (you and your partner) in Figure 5.1 are not positioned correctly. For example, you might say (and rightly so) that the two of you should shift a little bit to the left and reduce the width of region A. In doing so, it becomes more difficult for the opponent to hit a shot that is down the line. If you and your partner do shift a bit from the standard alignment shown in Figure 5.1, the regions A, B and C only change slightly, and such small modifications do not appreciably affect the following argument.

Now, I want to contrast the standard defensive alignment in Figure 5.1 with an alternative alignment proposed in Figure 5.2. This new alignment is the same as before except that the player marked with the dot on the right hand side of the court (say it is you) has dropped back 8.0 feet. Intuitively, this is a natural reaction. You are about to have the ball smashed back at you - therefore, you take a few steps back to give yourself more time to react. However, this new alignment does not conform to the standard principle that you and your partner are tethered together at roughly the same distance from the NVZ. In addition, you have dropped back and have entered the dreaded "no-man's land", a region on the court that is widely considered non-optimal. For example, when you are positioned in no-man's land, the opponent is more able to volley the shot at your left heel, which is a difficult location from which you can make a return. Therefore, conventional wisdom suggests that dropping back as illustrated in Figure 5.2 is not a good thing to do.

However, I would like to compare region B from both Figure 5.1 and Figure 5.2. Note that region B has completely disappeared in Figure 5.2! Therefore, the alternative positioning eliminates the middle gap where the opponent would prefer to hit the shot. This suggests that the alternative positioning in Figure 5.2 may be better than the advocated standard positioning in Figure 5.1 under the specific circumstances. Note that under the alternative positioning, region C could be made smaller while still eliminating region B if you move a little to the right.

There is an aspect of the alignment in Figure 5.2 which makes it even more preferable than the standard alignment in Figure 5.1. Recall that the opponent is about to hit a hard volley. You and your partner are in a vulnerable defensive situation. Being further back,

Chapter 5. Approaching the Net   41

you will have more time to react, and consequently, you can reach balls both further to the left and further to the right than would be possible in Figure 5.1. In other words, you will have an even wider effective wingspan than shown in Figure 5.2.

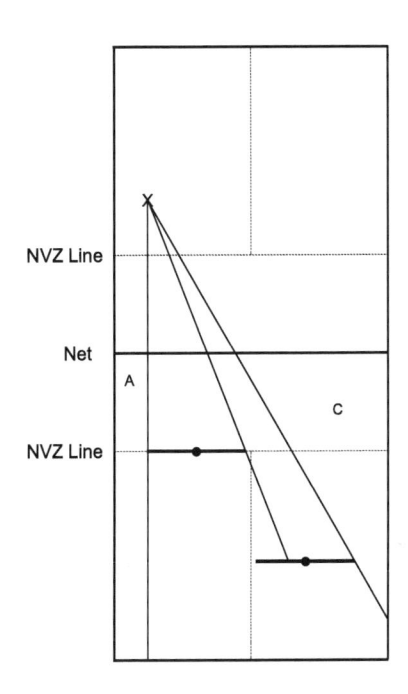

Figure 5.2: Gap regions A, B (disappeared) and C based on an alternative positioning proposal where the right court player (you, marked with a dot) has dropped back 8.0 feet from the standard positioning given in Figure 5.1. The symbol X denotes your opponent and the bolded lines depict the total wingspan of you and your partner.

The takeaway message is that general principles of strategy may not be optimal in every context. In this example, an important contextual feature is that you know that player X is going to hit the ball really hard. In this case, the alternative defensive alignment where you drop back as shown in Figure 5.2 is preferable to the standard alignment shown in Figure 5.1. This is an example where analytical thinking may assist in developing better strategies in particular circumstances. Don't blindly accept everything that you are told.

CHAPTER 6

The Banger

In some pickleball circles, "banger" has become a pejorative term. A banger is someone who hits the ball hard at most opportunities and is not seen as having the finesse of more accomplished pickleball players. I have been called a banger.

This very short chapter considers both the advantages and the disadvantages of banging. However, this is less of an analytics chapter, and consists mostly of opinions. I try to address some of the sentiments related to banging. In Chapter 15, probabilistic reasoning is used to compare the strategy of hitting the ball hard (i.e. banging) versus the strategy of hitting the third shot drop.

In pickleball, like most sports, players fall along a spectrum according to the degree that they embrace competition. By competition, I am not talking about the ability to play well, but the desire to win. I think that highly competitive players adopt more of a win at all costs attitude. I think that they are less bothered by the strategies of their opponents, as long as these strategies conform to the rules of play. The highly competitive player's primary objective is to overcome opponent strategies and simply win the game.

However, at the other end of the competitive spectrum, there are players who become upset when their opponents use particular strategies. For example, some players view lobbing as poor form. When you lob, your opponent may need to move backward, possibly

Chapter 6. The Banger

a dangerous maneuver for a less mobile player. With a lob, you may also require your opponent to look up in the sun, and this makes the return of the lob more difficult. As a second example, in close play at the net, there is the often the accidental byproduct of hitting an opponent with the ball. Often, this is followed by an apology since some players dislike being hit by the ball. However, hitting the opponent with the ball has also been suggested as a strategy - that is, something to be done intentionally. And although it may be viewed as poor form, intentionally hitting your opponent with the ball is within the formal rules of play, and it is definitely an effective strategy. When the ball comes to you quickly, towards the middle of your body and you cannot extend your paddle, you lose the point if it hits your body. I think that with many competitive players (especially those who have played physical sports), they react to being hit by the ball as no biggy, it's plastic, let's move on.

So, how does this relate to banging? It is my opinion that some players on the less competitive side of the spectrum also interpret banging as poor form. They see banging as "not nice". And I think the reason they don't like banging is because it is often difficult for them to handle such shots. They prefer to deal with shots that give them more time, and do not "scare" them. Personally, in a fun game, if I sense this attitude, I take my foot off the gas and try to keep everyone happy.

As a player, how can you counteract a banger? There are a few things that you can do. The banger is sometimes their worst enemy. Because they are hitting the ball hard, their ability to control the shot is less than if they hit it softer. Consequently, bangers will often hit shots into the net or out of bounds. So, I believe a counter-strategy against banging is to simply keep the ball in play - let the

Chapter 6. The Banger

banger make the mistake.

Obviously, as you give the banger better opportunities to hit the ball really hard (e.g. popped up shots), then it is more likely that they will be successful with their banging tactics. Shots that are low and barely clear the net are more difficult for the banger to hit hard (e.g. dink shots and drop shots). Another banging prevention shot is the lob serve (i.e. a serve with a higher arc than usual) which lands near the endline. In this case, the high bounce following the lob serve may be more difficult for the banger to hit hard. Actually, a lob shot at any point in a rally keeps the banger back and reduces their ability to bang effectively. It also allows your team time to advance to the non-volley zone if your lob is well executed.

It is also widely advised that a strategy against banging is to block the shot. That is, get your paddle in position, and simply direct it back. Since the banged ball was hit hard, your blocked shot will also have pace and cause difficulties for the banger. Furthermore, since the banger has flung their body to hit the shot hard, they may not be in a solid defensive position to handle your return block.

Now, as I have suggested, there are players who don't like to play against bangers. In turn, what they sometimes say is "banging won't work when you play against high-level players". Well, of course not, and I think this sentiment misses the point. Nothing works well when you play against high-level players. That is why they are high-level players. What is relevant is whom you are playing against at the moment; not future hypothetical high-level players. The real question, if you are competive and your main desire is to win, is whether banging is a good strategy for you in a particular situation against particular players. I suggest that to evaluate this properly requires a probabilistic approach as demonstrated in Chapter 15.

Chapter 6. The Banger

I have one more comment concerning banging that lies on the obvious side. For anyone, time is of the essence in pickleball. The less time that is available to hit a shot, the more difficult it becomes to hit the shot. Therefore, if you are going to bang, bang hard which gives your opponent less time. But do keep your shot in play. And the closer you are to the non-volley zone when you bang, the less time is afforded to your opponents.

Chapter 7

Unforced Errors

I believe that the reduction of unforced errors provides the greatest opportunity in pickleball for players to improve their game.

I want to begin with a discussion of what is meant by an unforced error. In two words, an unforced error is a *dumb mistake*. It is mistake that is avoidable and completely of your own doing. Nobody causes an unforced error other than you. An indisputable example of an unforced error is a serve that you hit out of bounds. The opponent has nothing to do with your serve; the mistake is completely on you.

Although the term unforced error may not be widely familiar, everybody knows what it is. When a player makes an unforced error, they often just shake their head in shame. What most players don't know is the rate that they make unforced errors. It may be that 20% of your shots are unforced errors and that 30% of my shots are unforced errors.

So, why then do players not obtain their personal unforced error rate, and work on reducing their rate? If your rate is high compared to your competitors, this is a great avenue for personal improvement. Players could even isolate their unforced errors. For example, it would be instructive to know your unforced error rate when serving, when dinking, when lobbing, etc. You could then monitor your rates over time and see if your game is improving.

Although possible, there are several obstacles in calculating your

Chapter 7. Unforced Errors

unforced error rate. If you had a friend sitting courtside, they would need to count your unforced errors and your total number of touches. Your unforced error rate would then be your number of unforced errors divided by your total number of touches. The friend would need to do this over many games; you would need to have a very good friend. A problem with having your friend count unforced errors is that the game is very fast. It would be challenging to obtain accurate counts. A solution, although not available to everyone, and perhaps impractical, is to record videos of your matches. Then, you don't need your friend. You can go home, and do the counting yourself.

The second obstacle in the determination of unforced error rates is subjectivity. For example, suppose that you hit the third shot of the rally into the net. Was this completely your fault, i.e. an unforced error? Or did your opponent hit such a good second shot that it was nearly impossible for you to return, and you hit it into the net, i.e. a forced error? Clearly, the quality of your opponents' shots is related to the determination of whether or not you made an unforced error.

Although I have expressed challenges in the accurate calculation of unforced error rates, I do not think these challenges are insurmountable. Certainly, for professional players, it is possible. Video is available. All that is needed is a workable definition of an unforced error such that unforced errors can be counted objectively. For those of us who are not professionals, we are likely going to need to wait for technology to change the landscape with respect to the calculation of unforced error rates. But even if you do not know your unforced error rates, you likely have a feeling whether you commit unforced errors more or less frequently than your competitors.

Now, let's assume for the moment that we knew our overall un-

Chapter 7. Unforced Errors

forced error rate. And let's assume further that we could reduce our rate by 10%. We would then like to know how much our game would improve. A difficulty in determining the effect of an unforced error is that we do not know the way that a rally would have played out had the unforced error not occurred. This is referred to as a *counterfactual* situation, and I believe that this is a reason why the sports analytics literature concerning unforced errors is sparse. However, there has been some recent work in tennis[1] that addresses counterfactuals involving unforced errors. To my knowledge, there is nothing out there on unforced errors in pickleball. Therefore, we are going to look at the state of affairs in tennis to provide us with some insight on unforced errors in pickleball.

I hypothesize that there are more unforced errors in pickleball than there are in tennis. This is because the tennis court is much larger than the pickleball court. Therefore, in tennis, there are many more shots that are unreachable than in pickleball. The loss of a rally due to an unreachable shot is not an unforced error; there is nothing you can do about a shot you cannot reach. Therefore, whatever we see in tennis with respect to unforced errors, you can imagine that the negative consequence of unforced errors in pickleball is even more severe.

In the aforementioned article, a study was done on the impact of unforced errors between Roger Federer and Rafael Nadal during their long and storied rivalry. They competed 40 times against one another during their careers with Federer winning 16 of the matches, and winning 49.3% of the points. In their recorded matches, Federer had an unforced error rate of 8.9% and Nadal had an unforced error

---

[1] Peiris, H., Epasinghege Dona, N. and Swartz, T.B. (2024). Analysis of the impact of unforced errors in tennis. https://arxiv.org/abs/2407.19321.

rate of 5.7%. Again, keep in mind that these are two of the greatest tennis players of all time, with low unforced error rates compared to what mid-level players would exhibit in pickleball.

The article then carries out a counterfactual analysis to investigate how much better Federer would have performed had he been able to reduce his unforced error rate by 10% (i.e. from 8.9% to 8.0%). In this case, Federer would still have a higher unforced error rate than Nadal but this would represent an improvement for Federer. Using a *bootstrapping* technique, the paper suggests that the "improved Federer" would have won 50.3% of the points, and won approximately 21.5 of the 40 matches. Had Federer been able to improve his unforced error rate by only 10%, there would perhaps be a different narrative concerning their generational rivalry.

As of today, we do not know a lot about personal unforced error rates in pickleball. However, by a comparison with the sister sport of tennis, there is a case to be made that great improvements can be realized in pickleball via the reduction of unforced errors. If you are a mid-level player, the chances are that you make a significant number of unforced errors, and this provides a great opportunity for you to improve your game. High level pickleball players also make unforced errors; however, I suspect such errors are made at a lower rate.

CHAPTER 8

The Bucket - Predictability

There is a wonderful guy at the pickleball club where I play. For the sake of this chapter, let's call him "Pickleball Joe". Pickleball Joe is a good player, but most importantly to me, he is encouraging. He gives lessons and always has some pickleball wisdom in his back pocket. If it wasn't for Pickleball Joe, I likely would not have taken up the game.

Well, one of Pickleball Joe's favorite sayings is to "drop the ball in the white bucket". What he means by this is that when both teams have advanced near the non-volley zone (NVZ), the ideal spot to place your dink shot is in the imaginary bucket depicted in Figure 8.1. This assumes that the receiving player (marked with an x in the diagram) is right-handed. Pickleball Joe says that we are to do this whether we are on the right side or the left side of the court. Dropping the ball in the white bucket is an appealing mnemonic for a beginner since it is easy to remember and sounds so easy to do.

In Figure 8.1, you see that the dink shot is directed to the opponent's backhand. The majority of players are weaker on their backhand than on their forehand, and therefore, it is more likely that your opponent will mess up if your dink shot is dropped in the white bucket rather than dropped in some other location. Pickleball Joe goes on to say that you should be patient, and continue to drop the ball in the white bucket, waiting for your opponent to make a

Chapter 8. The Bucket - Predictability

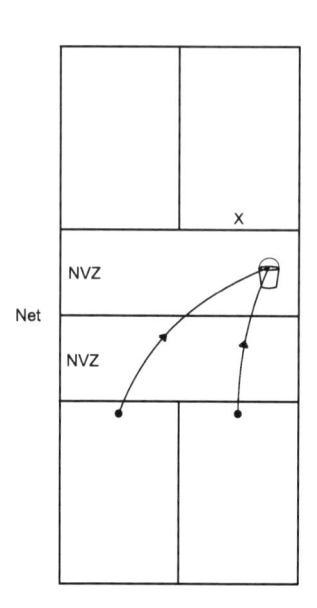

Figure 8.1: The imaginary bucket indicates the ideal location for dropping dink shots to a right-handed player (marked with an x). The two dots indicate arbitrary locations from where the player may hit a dink shot.

mistake. For example, the opponent may eventually hit the ball into the net. Or possibly, the opponent may eventually pop the ball up, giving you an opportunity to volley it back with pace and direct the ball towards an advantageous location.

All of this sounds sensible, and generally speaking, I think that sensible rules of thumb should be followed *most of the time*. According to Pickleball Joe, the purpose of dropping the ball in the white bucket is to get "the new player to slow down and be more patient".

However, there is an aspect to strategy which I would like to discuss. The main message is that as a pickleball player, you should not be predictable. In the case of dropping the ball in the white bucket, once in a while you should do something else (preferably

Chapter 8. The Bucket - Predictability

something good) so that your opponent needs to be on their toes. If they know exactly what you are about to do, then they can prepare and possibly exploit the situation. Of course, Pickleball Joe knows this.

The advice about avoiding predictability applies to many aspects of pickleball (e.g. the nature of your serve, whether you hit a third shot drop, whether you lob, whether you spin the ball, etc.). The first question then is what are the possible alternative strategies that you should consider if you wish to be less predictable. Whether a strategy is good depends on various factors including your skill level of executing various shots and the quality of your opponents. In Part III of the book, we develop a general approach where you can assess your personal pickleball strategies.

At this point, you may be wondering about the downside of being predictable. There is a great interview on youtube[1] where the tennis legend Andre Agassi explains how he enjoyed success against another tennis legend, Boris Becker. Agassi describes that Becker had a terrific serve and defeated Agassi in their first three matches. However, from watching film, Agassi discovered that Becker inadvertently signaled the direction of his serves by sticking out his tongue, either to the side or to the middle. Agassi kept this a secret, but profited from Becker's predictability, and defeated Becker in 9 of their next 11 matches. After revealing the secret to Becker in their retirement, Becker commented that it was though Agassi could read my mind.

This leads to a difficult question involving predictability that I now wish to address: how should you vary your strategies to avoid being predictable? The proper solution to this problem utilizes *game*

---
[1] See https://www.youtube.com/watch?v=ja6HeLB3kwY

theory, a mathematical/economics topic that is beyond the scope of this book. In the remainder of this chapter, we explore the mixing of strategies as suggested by game theory in three disparate domains of study.

8.1 Mixing Strategies in Other Domains

Example (i): Let's first discuss the popular children's game Rock-Paper-Scissors. In the game, both children simultaneously make a gesture of either a rock, paper or scissors. If one child shows rock and the other child shows scissors, then rock defeats scissors. If one child shows scissors and the other child shows paper, then scissors defeats paper. If one child shows paper and the other child shows rock, then paper defeats rock. If both children make the same gesture, then neither child wins; the game is drawn. In this game, neither child has an advantage if they both choose from their three gestures randomly, each gesture with probability 1/3.

Now, for simplicity, assume that one child is completely predictable. Call this child P, for predictable. For example, P always chooses scissors. Then, recognizing the pattern, child C (the clever one), always chooses rock. Thus, C wins all the time. The obvious point is that you should not be predictable.

The predictability issue also extends from being completely predictable to being partially predictable. For example, suppose P instead chooses scissors with probability 1/2 and chooses paper with probability 1/2. With this pattern, P never chooses rock, and therefore, P is partially predictable. Note that P is behaving randomly, but this is also not a good approach. In this case, C again recognizes the pattern, and by being clever, C always chooses scissors. In this case, C never loses; C draws 1/2 of the time corresponding to when P choose scissors and C wins 1/2 of the time corresponding to when P chooses paper.

So, in the Rock-Paper-Scissors example, we see that it is a disadvantage when you are completely predictable or even partially predictable.

Example (ii): Let's now consider a fictitious foreign policy situation involving a world leader. Perhaps the world leader wants to accomplish something unpopular and has nuclear weapons at their disposal. Will any nation oppose this leader with respect to the unpopular behavior? If the leader is seen as rational, then nations may oppose the leader since they do not fear the retaliation of nuclear weapons. No rational leader would respond with nuclear weapons over a minor issue given that the consequences of the nuclear option are so dire. In this case, being rational implies being predictable. However, if the leader is irrational and hence unpredictable, then nations may be less likely to oppose the leader for fear of nuclear retaliation.

Therefore, in world politics, being viewed as unpredictable may confer a weird advantage. It might be better that leaders mix their strategies. Actually, such a leader does not actually have to be unpredictable, but rather, they only need to exude the impression of being unpredictable. Maybe this is why some of our leaders behave the way that they do :)

Example (iii): For a more detailed example of mixing strategies, consider penalty kicks in the beautiful game (i.e. soccer). Given that soccer matches are low-scoring with fewer than three goals per game on average in the top leagues, and given that penalty kicks are scored at a high rate (roughly 75% successful), penalty kicks are often influential in terms of match results.

We will assume that there are three types of penalty kicks according to the direction that they are taken: left (L), right (R) and down the middle (M). See Figure 8.2 for illustration of the three scenarios.

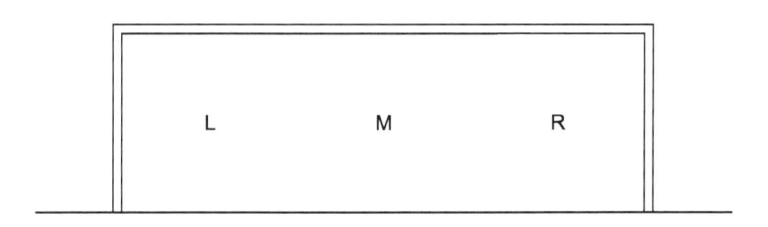

Figure 8.2: A soccer goal depicting the three regions where penalty kicks may be taken. We denote these regions L - left, M - middle and R - right.

Given that penalty kicks can reach the keeper quickly (e.g. as fast as 0.2 seconds), there is little time for the keeper to react. Hence, it is common for the keeper to guess where the penalty kick will be directed, and accordingly, the keeper will make a decision to move before the ball is kicked. Hence, immediately prior the ball being kicked, the keeper will begin moving to L or R, or remain in the M position. And typically, the kicker will not have time to judge which way the keeper will move, and therefore, the kicker will also make a decision regarding the intended direction of the kick, L, R or M. Consequently, we think of the two actions (by the keeper and the kicker) as occurring simultaneously without the input of clues from each other. As you can see, this is a sporting situation involving predictability between the two contestants, the keeper and the kicker. Each is trying to guess what the other is about to do.

Chapter 8. The Bucket - Predictability

To determine the "best" strategies for the keeper and the kicker, game theory is utilized where the main objective of both parties is to avoid being exploited. In order to derive these strategies, the starting point is Table 8.1. In Table 8.1, I provide the percentages that goals are scored according to the 9 possible situations based on where the kicker aims (three choices L,M,R) and where the keeper moves (three choices L,M,R). For example, in Table 8.1, if the kicker aims left (L) and the the keeper moves right (R), a goal will be scored 95% of the time. This is a high percentage where the only occasion that a goal is not scored (5% of the time) occurs when the kicker misses the net by either shooting wide or shooting high.

Kicker Direction	Keeper Direction L	M	R
L	60%	93%	95%
M	90%	3%	90%
R	95%	93%	60%

Table 8.1: Percentages of occasions where a goal is scored according to the 9 possible penalty kick scenarios determined by the kicker's aim and the keeper's movement.

Now, I want to emphasize that the entries in Table 8.1 are estimates; the true percentages are unknown. The estimates are obtained from past data involving penalty kicks. Also, in deriving these estimates, I have made various assumptions including symmetry between left and right footedness, and the lack of consideration of stuttered[2] penalty kicks. Table 8.1 is a necessary ingredient for the subsequent game theory analysis. I mention that alternative es-

---

[2] A stuttered penalty kick is one where the kicker's approach to the ball involves slowing down (feinting but not completely stopping) so as to entice the keeper to reveal their movement.

timates to those shown in Table 8.1 have been obtained by other researchers[3] but these do not seem to differ greatly from the entries in Table 8.1.

And finally, here is the main result which is derived as a consequence of the entries in Table 8.1: the mixed-strategy Nash equilibrium solution is given in Table 8.2. Obviously, this is a technical statement. However, the bottom line is quite simple. If the kicker wants to behave optimally, then they should aim at the locations L, M and R with percentages 42.4%, 15.1% and 42.4%, respectively. If the keeper wants to behave optimally, then they should move to the locations L, M and R with percentages 43.9%, 12.2% and 43.9%, respectively. Moreover, in professional soccer, it appears that kickers and keepers make decisions that approximately conform to these percentages. Therefore, they are making nearly optimal decisions in practice.

	L	M	R
Kicker Aims	42.4%	15.1%	42.4%
Keeper Moves	43.9%	12.2%	43.9%

Table 8.2: Mixed-strategy Nash equilibrium solution for penalty kicks based on the entries in Table 8.1. The percentages for the kicker correspond to the frequency with which they should aim for L, M and R. The percentages for the keeper correspond to the frequency with which they should move to the locations L, M and R.

The most interesting aspect about the results given in Table 8.2, and the takeaway message, is that the kicker and the keeper have random strategies. They choose one of their three actions according to the given percentages. Thus, their actions are not predictable.

---
[3]Azar, O.H. and Bar-Eli, M. (2011). Do soccer players play the mixed-strategy Nash equilibrium? Applied Economics, 43(25), 3591-3601.

Chapter 8. The Bucket - Predictability

So, we have seen from both a common sense point of view, and from high level mathematics that being predictable is not advantageous in various practical domains.

Now, how can we relate all of this to the pickleball strategy of dropping the ball in the white bucket? Suppose that you were completely predictable and that you always attempted to drop the ball in the white bucket according to Figure 8.1. I suggest that if you did this all of the time (or nearly all of the time), your opponent would begin to take notice. And to make things easier for your opponent, they might shift a little bit from location x1 to location x2 as indicated in Figure 8.3. If your opponent made this shift, then your drop shots in the white bucket would instead be on the opponent's forehand, and your original advantage would disappear. Of course, in turn, you would begin to notice that the opponent shifted their position, and you would observe a larger gap between your two opponents. In this case, it would then make sense for you to hit the ball down the middle occasionally instead of dropping the ball in the white bucket all of the time. Changing your tactics from being completely predictable will prevent your opponent from taking advantage of you.

Avoiding predictability arises not only in the white bucket example, but in many situations in pickleball. For example, it makes sense to vary your serve, and you can do so in many ways. You can vary your serve left to right, short or long, with different spins, with more or less speed, and with degrees of arc.

In conclusion, as seen in the white bucket example, you want to keep your opponent on their toes. You do not want them to know exactly what you are about to do since such knowledge provides them with a competitive advantage. Therefore, you need to mix it

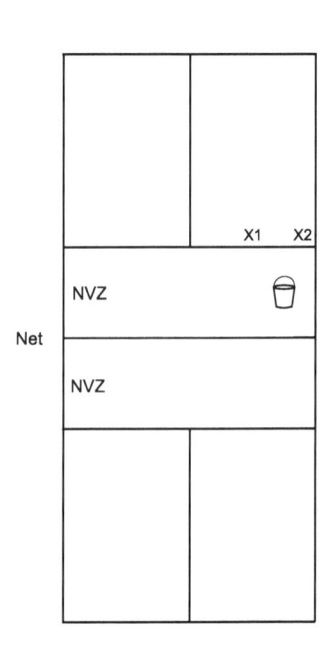

Figure 8.3: The imaginary bucket indicates the recommended location for dink shots to a right-handed player. In the diagram, we indicate how the opponent (marked with x1) might shift to a new position x2 if they were sure that every shot were dropped in the white bucket.

up a bit (i.e. randomize) so that the opponent is unsure what you are going to do next. The minute you see the opponent anticipating what you are about to do, you are likely becoming predictable, and it is probably a good time to mix your strategies.

Not being predictable sounds like common sense. But it is easy to become predictable, and as a pickleball player, you should be wary of falling into this trap. If you become predictable, it is possible to be exploited.

Chapter 9

Playing in the Wind

Many of us have developed a habit of paying attention to weather forecasts. Temperature and precipitation have an impact on how we carry out our lives. Now that I have become a pickleball player, I have also started to check the wind forecast for outdoor play. Naturally, the pickleball is affected by the wind since it is very light (less than one ounce). I have found that windspeeds above 10 mph (16 kmph) begin to impact my play. For instantaneous assessments, I have become adept at estimating windspeed by looking at my neighbor's flag.

Apart from my preference to play during calm days, how should you adjust your game during windy days? There is some common sense advice to minimize the impact of the wind. For example, topspin shots are recommended since the spin drives your shot towards the ground, and consequently, the ball spends less time in the wind. In addition, you might avoid lob shots (which are high) since they are more difficult to control in the wind. There is also advice that you should play closer to the non-volley zone since this reduces the time that your shots are airborne. Of course, the last point is not a great revelation since it is generally recommended to play close to the non-volley zone, wind or no wind.

The best common sense advice is simple - be aware of the wind. For example, it is good to understand the extent to which a left-to-

Chapter 9. Playing in the Wind

right wind will pull your shots to the right. Assessing the impact of the wind when it is swirling is obviously more difficult.

I want to focus on a narrow question: is it better to play with the wind or play against the wind? And I would like to restrict our attention to moderately windy situations, say between 10 mph and 20 mph. Beyond that, playing conditions tend to become silly. The question of wind direction is important since you may be given a choice of ends. Therefore, making the correct choice of ends may confer a competitive advantage with respect to the wind.

There is no consensus opinion whether it is better to play with or against the wind. Some players prefer playing with the wind, as explained in a book[1] on pickleball strategy - "A heavy wind at your back is an advantage to a hard hitter because it could add 15-20 mph to their stroke, making it much harder for their opponent to react".

I do believe that when you are smashing the ball, it is an advantage to play with the wind. By smashing, I mean hitting the ball from a high impact point, say 7 feet above the ground, and hitting the ball with a downward trajectory. With smashes, we tend to hit the ball nearly as hard as we can, and playing with the wind simply makes the smash faster and more challenging than if you are playing against the wind. But keep in mind that smashes do not occur all of the time; they happen far less frequently than drop shots and drives, for example. Therefore, we are not going to be greatly concerned with smashes in developing an overall recommendation to play with or against the wind.

As for the short game, I think that there are only minor differ-

---

[1] See page 211 in Movsessian, R. and Baker, J. (2018). How to Play Pickleball: The Complete Guide from A to Z. ISBN-13: 978-1-7239-9308-4.

Chapter 9. Playing in the Wind

ences between playing with the wind and playing against the wind. When you are close to the net and hitting soft shots, the ball is not in the air for great distances, and therefore, moderate winds only have a small impact on the flight of the ball.

The shot that I would like to focus on is the common drive shot. Is it better to play with the wind or play against the wind when hitting drive shots? Let's use some analytics of projectile motion to provide a perspective on the question.

Projectile motion is a complex topic, too mathematical for detailed presentation in this chapter. Projectile motion depends on various ambient factors including the wind velocity and gravity. Projectile motion also depends on characteristics of the projectile including the launch velocity, the launch height, the launch angle and the impact of air resistance which in turn depends on the weight, size, shape, surface and spin of the projectile. Applications in projectile motion not only concern our sporting question but also very serious areas of inquiry such as ballistics.

Despite the mathematical complexity of projectile motion, we present some simple insights related to the flight of a pickleball that are accurate, at least on a qualitative scale. There exists some technical research[2] upon which our insights are based.

We consider a pickleball that is struck from the middle of the left side of the court at a particular launch angle (20 degrees with respect to the horizon) and from a 3-foot height. This type of shot is considered a drive. If you are a highly skilled pickleball player, your launch angle is likely less than 20 degrees; you need to balance the benefit of a flatter and lower shot against the possibility of hitting

---

[2] Emonds, K., Sun, W. and Swartz, T.B. (2024). Pickleball flight dynamics. https://doi.org/10.51224/SRXIV.456

Chapter 9. Playing in the Wind

the ball into the net. The ball is struck according to four winds speeds: $w = -10$ mph (against the wind), $w = 0$ mph (no wind), $w = 10$ mph (with the wind) and $w = 15$ mph (with the wind). We further assume that the pickleball is hit with such a force that its initial velocity, together with gravity, air resistance and windspeed cause the pickleball to land at the endline on the right hand side of the court.

Now, in many circumstances, this would be an ideal drive shot, hitting the ball deep to your opponents' court. This is a key assumption in the following argumentation. In a comparison of the "with wind" shot versus the "against wind" shot, you are going to hit the best possible shot in both wind contexts - a shot that if left untouched, would bounce in play, near the endline. We are going to make the assumption that as a player, you have the ability to hit this type of shot. Clearly, to accomplish this, you will need to hit the ball harder when the wind is against you. Therefore, and keep this in mind - the pickleball will have a greater initial velocity when you are playing against the wind than when you are playing with the wind.

In Figure 9.1, we plot the path of the pickleball under the four windspeeds. We observe that the trajectories for wind speeds $w = 0, 10, 15$ mph do not differ greatly. However, when playing against the wind (i.e. $w = -10$ mph), the pickleball flight has a greater curvature with a higher arc. It appears that the pickleball gets held up by the wind. This is something that all pickleballers know. Towards the end of the flight path when playing against the wind, the pickleball is moving more in a downward direction than a horizontal direction.

We have studied the path of the pickleball when playing with

Chapter 9. Playing in the Wind

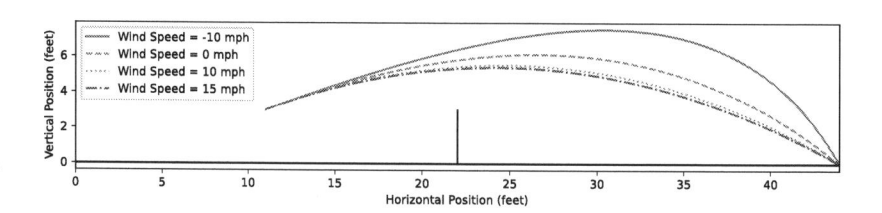

Figure 9.1: Trajectory of the pickleball in four wind conditions $w = -10$ mph, $w = 0$ mph, $w = 10$ mph and $w = 15$ mph according to the assumptions described above.

and against the wind. Let's return to the question of whether it is better to play with the wind or against the wind. Suppose that you hit the shot as described above (i.e. as hard as needed to reach the endline) in the two situations, with the wind and against the wind. I am interested in the time that it takes the pickleball to reach your opponent. Here is the important result according to pickleball flight dynamics: in most circumstances, the pickleball will reach your opponent sooner when you are playing against the wind. Therefore, when playing against the wind, your opponent will have less time to react, and this will make the return shot more difficult for them. And the harder the wind blows, the advantage increases when playing against the wind versus playing with the wind. The only time the above result is not true is when your opponent is sitting far back, near their endline; and recall, this is not a generally recommended strategy in pickleball.

In summary, we have considered a common situation in pickleball where the ball is hit hard, i.e. a drive. In this situation, given that you hit the ideal drive shot, some theory from projectile motion demonstrates that it is better to play against the wind than with the wind.

Moreover, there are at least two additional advantages when playing against the wind. First, if you like to bang the ball, you have less to worry about when you are playing against the wind; you can hit the ball hard and it is less likely to go out of bounds. Second, the important third shot drop (or any drop shot for that matter) is easier to execute against the win than with the wind. When you hit the third shot drop, you need to be concerned with two things: (1) hitting the ball short and into the net, and (2) hitting the ball a bit high such that it is smashed back at you. When you are playing against the win, you don't need to be as concerned with point (2). Your third shot drop will get pushed down by the wind.

Chapter 10

Variability and Winning

What are you to do when playing pickleball and you are facing superior competition? Lay down and die? I don't think so.

As discussed in Chapter 7, upsets do occur in pickleball, and they occur with some regularity. However, are there some specific things that you can do to improve your chance of winning?

The situation that interests me is not the case where you are mildly outmatched; say you win 40% of the time. In these situations, I recommend that you play as well as you can, and if you play well or get lucky, there is still a good chance that you can win.

Instead, I am looking at situations where you are a major underdog, say with only a 10% chance of winning. If you stick to the same old, same old routine and perform at your typical level, you are not likely to come out on top. Your opponents will just grind your team down according to their superior ability.

I am interested in ways in which you can slightly improve your chances of winning in situations where you are badly outmatched. By doing something radical, you may actually lose by more points than if you played your standard game. However, the objective is to win, especially in a single match. It does not really matter if you lose 11-4 or 11-2.

What I want to discuss is the introduction of additional variability into the match. This general idea was discussed in a journal article[1] in the sport of Twenty20 cricket.

The sorts of things that I have in mind to increase variability concern changes in strategy. You should implement tactics, that if executed correctly, your opponents can do little about. I recommend that you do fewer things that allow their superiority to take over. For example, here are some ideas that you may consider:

- Hit a few more shots down the line. If you are successful and execute a great line shot, then you will likely win the rally. It does not really matter if your opponents are great players; they will be unable to reach your line shot.

- In the dinking phase of a rally, eventually the game gets sped up. When dinking, your team should more often be the team to speed up the game. For example, you might consider hitting a hard volley when the dink is just a little bit high. If you execute it well, there is not much that your opponents can do about it, and you will win the rally.

- You may consider trying some of your lesser used serves. You may catch your opponents off guard and they may struggle with the return.

- You may consider some offensive lobs. Again, you may catch your opponents off guard.

In general, you can increase variability by playing more aggressively and taking more risks. Another way of thinking about this is to alter your style so that some of your rally outcomes go from good to great, although other outcomes may go from bad to terrible. For

---

[1]Silva, R., Perera, H., Davis, J. and Swartz, T.B. (2016). Tactics for Twenty20 cricket. South African Statistical Journal, 50(2), 261-271.

Chapter 10. Variability and Winning

example, you may try to hit a fancy serve close to a boundary. A good shot may land in play, one foot from the boundary. A great shot would land in play, one inch from the boundary. On the other hand, a bad serve may be one foot out of bounds, and a terrible shot may be 5 feet out of bounds. So, not much is really lost. When trying to win rallies, there is often little practical difference between bad and terrible.

In Figure 10.1, we use the simulator discussed earlier (see Section 3.4) to produce histograms of score differentials based on 10,000 hypothetical matches. Here, we define score differential as the number of points that the better team defeats the weaker team. For example, if the better team wins 11-6, the score differential is 5. On the other hand, if the weaker team wins 11-9, the score differential is -2. Note that on the horizontal axis, score differentials of -1, 0 and 1 are impossible in pickleball since the rules do not allow ties and the winner must win by at least two points. In Figure 10.1, the degree of mismatch between the weaker team and the stronger team has been coded such that the weaker team wins only 40% of the rallies. However, with the generic simulator, we can simulate matches and produce histograms for any specified degree of mismatch.

Consider the top histogram in Figure 10.1. The height of a bar on the histogram depicts the frequency of the event on the horizontal axis. For example, a score differential of 11 on the horizontal axis means that the weaker team was "pickled" and lost 11-0. Here, we observe that the corresponding bar has a height of roughly 600. That means that the weaker team is pickled only 6% of the time (600 times out of the 10,000 simulations).

Let's look at another event from the top histogram in Figure 10.1. A score differential of -3 from the horizontal axis means that the weaker team won by 3 points. We see that the height of the corresponding bar is a little greater than 100. This means that the weaker team wins by exactly 3 points a little more than 1% of the time (100 times out of the 10,000 simulations). The histogram describes the frequency of score differentials that would be expected between two teams had they played many times.

There are two additional features in the top histogram which I would like to draw to your attention. First, the median score differential is 6. This means that half the time the weaker team loses by 6 points (e.g. 11-5) or by more points, and half the time they do better than that. This emphasizes that the contest is a considerable mismatch. The other prominent feature concerns the histogram bars $-2, -3, \ldots, -11$. These are the bars that correspond to the simulations where the weaker team actually wins the match. Adding up the heights of these bars, it turns out that the weaker team wins only 9% of the time.

Now, I would like you to focus on the bottom histogram in Figure 10.1. This is the context where the outmatched team adds additional variability to their playing style. As previously discussed, the outmatched team introduces more aggressive tactics.

The bottom histogram looks very similar to the top histogram except that variability has slightly increased. In other words, the bars are more spread out; wins for the stronger team become bigger wins and losses for the stronger team become bigger losses. In the bottom histogram, the median score differential remains at 6 points, meaning that the degree of the mismatch between the two teams is the same as before. However, what is meaningful is that the histogram bars $-2, -3, \ldots, -11$ now correspond to an overall win percentage of 13%. Therefore, by having the weaker team modify

Chapter 10. Variability and Winning

their tactics and increase their variability, the weaker team is able to increase their win percentage from 9% to 13%. It may not seem like a lot in absolute terms, but the change from 9% to 13% corresponds to a 44% increase.

The takeaway message in this chapter is that when your team is badly outmatched, you are likely going to lose. That's life. However, why not go for it? Mix things up and take some chances. Hit that wonder shot. Be less predictable. Increase your variability. You may lose by more points than if you played conservatively, but you will also slightly increase your chance of winning the match. Isn't that what you want to do?

Chapter 10. Variability and Winning

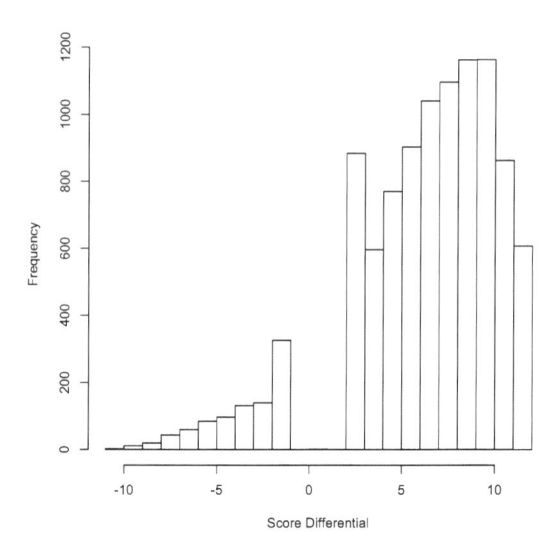

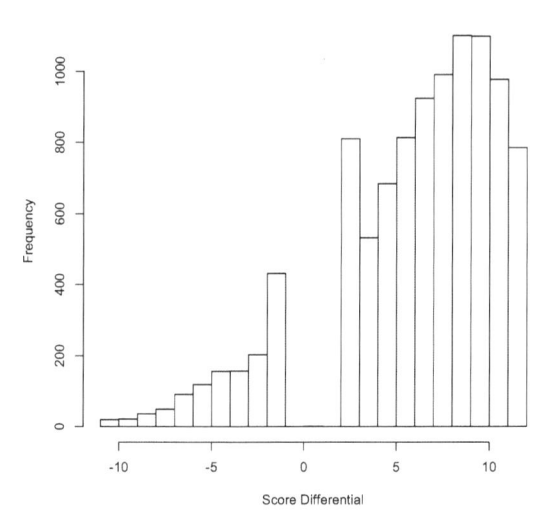

Figure 10.1: Histograms of the score of the stronger team less the score of the weaker team. In the bottom figure, there is slightly more variability in the score differentials than in the top figure.

Chapter 11

Pickleball and Longevity

This short chapter concerns strategy only in the broadest sense. The purported strategy is this: play pickleball and live a long life.

In 2017, an article[1] was published in the British Journal of Sports Medicine that looked at the relationship between sports participation and mortality amongst a large sample of British adults. The paper used careful language, and concluded that participation in racquet sports (badminton, tennis and squash) was *associated* with lower mortality.

In the aftermath, the journal article received a lot of attention. In particular, a number of related investigations have since been carried out. Also, in the public sphere, news agencies including the New York Times picked up on the research and began writing about the health benefits of particular sports. A quick Google search of sports participation and longevity indicates that the topic continues to be fashionable.

With the increasing popularity of pickleball, some of the benefits reported in the study (associated with racquet sports) have subsequently been endowed on pickleball.

The problem with many of the news stories is that they did not use the same careful language as in the original journal publication.

---

[1] Oja, P. et al. (2017). Associations of specific types of sports and exercise with all-cause and cardiovascular-disease mortality: a cohort study of 80306 British adults. British Journal of Sports Medicine, 51(10), 812-817.

Chapter 11. Pickleball and Longevity

Rather than discuss the association between sports participation and mortality, quotes began to appear such as "playing tennis extends one's life expectancy by 9.7 years"[2]. These statements, as much as pickleballers would like to believe them, confuse the notions of "association" and "cause and effect".

To see the false equivalency between association and cause and effect, let's consider an example where the distinction is clear. Accordingly, suppose that we are interested in two teaching methods, online instruction and in-class instruction. We would like to know which method is superior in terms of test results. Therefore, students at school A were given online instruction and students at school B were given in-class instruction. After a period of time, tests were administered and it was observed that school A (utilizing online instruction) performed better. Therefore, in this study, online instruction was *associated* with better test results. However, can we conclude that online instruction is the superior teaching method? In other words, is there a cause and effect relationship in the sense that online instruction caused better test results? We need to hold on. It could be that school A had better students to begin with, and they would have realized better test results under any method of instruction. Here, student quality is *confounded* with the instructional method, and student quality impacts test results.

A traditional way to identify cause and effect relationships is via randomized experiments. In the example, we could have instead grouped all students from both schools and randomly assigned each student to one of the two instructional methods. By randomizing students to the two methods of instruction, both methods would

---
[2] See www.forbes.com/sites/stevensalzberg/2018/09/17/want-to-live-longer-take-up-tennis/

Chapter 11. Pickleball and Longevity

have similar students on average. Then any observed difference between the test results of the two methods would be entirely due to the method of instruction and not to the inherent abilities of the students. It is through randomization that we are best able to assess cause and effect relationships.

Now, back to pickleball and longevity. It could be that health is a confounding variable. If you are not sufficiently healthy, you are not likely to play pickleball. And if you are not sufficiently healthy, you are not likely to have a long life. Therefore, health is confounded with playing pickleball, and health impacts longevity. In other words, perhaps it is mostly healthy people that play pickleball, and this is the reason that they live a long life - because they are initially healthy.

As a technical note, the original study introduced some variables (i.e. covariates) in their regression analyses that are associated with health. This is useful in mitigating the confounding effects relative to health. However, there may still be missing covariates in the study that are impactful in assessing cause and effect. For example, the study concerned six activities: racquet sports, cycling, swimming, aerobics, running, and soccer. In this list, I observed that the only activities which are primarily competitive are the racquet sports. Even soccer (which is seemingly competitive) most likely consists of less structured "kick-around" games since the mean age of the participants is 52 years. This suggests that mobility which is not considered in the list of covariates may be a confounding variable with health. Racquet sport players are likely more mobile than those in the other activities since it would not be enjoyable to play competitive racquet sports if mobility was a challenge. And it may be that mobility[3] is also an indicator of longevity. This is just one hypothesized confounder; there may be other missing variables in the study that are confounded with health.

So, it is reasonable to ask why don't researchers introduce randomization in a pickleball/longevity study. The reason is that it is impractical and possibly unethical. It is unlikely that you can obtain a sample of people, and then randomize them into two groups, saying to individuals, you must play pickleball or you cannot play pickleball.

Here are two additional doubts concerning the inferred 10-year lifespan benefit from playing pickleball:

- An extra 10 years is a long time. In fact, the standard deviation of life expectancy is only 8 years. Therefore, adding 10 years to the average life expectancy would place you in the top 10% of lifespans. That would be a remarkable consequence from smacking around a wiffle ball several times a week.

- There is no apparent physical explanation as to why pickleball (racquet sports in the study) should be so much better than cycling, swimming, aerobics, running and soccer.

Therefore, although the benefits of pickleball are indisputable, and include social and health aspects, I think you should play because you enjoy pickleball. The idea that you can add 10 years onto your life by beginning now, is a bit of a stretch.

---

[3]Nocera, J. et al. (2011). The impact of behavioral intervention on obesity mediated declines in mobility function: Implications for longevity. Journal of Aging Research, Article ID 392510.

Part III

PERSONAL STRATEGIES

I have left Part III to the end of the book. On a technical level, it is the most challenging section, but it may also be the most rewarding.

I hope that you will take some time with Chapter 12 and familiarize yourself with probability. This may require reading Chapter 12 multiple times. But if you can do that, and assign personal probabilities, then you will be able to determine pickleball strategies that are best for you!

And then, having obtained your optimal pickleball strategies, the results may help you target parts of your game for improvement.

Chapters 13-15 have a similar feel; once you master one of the chapters, you will have understood the general approach. In the future, if you are faced with a fresh pickleball problem where you need to decide between competing strategies, the general approach developed here is applicable.

CHAPTER 12

Probability

If you have ever taken a course in Statistics, beware, some of those memories may return.

However, I am only going to introduce the necessary material, and from scratch. I am also going to present the material in a simple manner and relate theoretical concepts to familiar situations.

Unfortunately, probability theory is *tricky*. Actually, it is more than that - probability theory is difficult. For starters, there are various definitions of probability, most of which are unsatisfactory in one way or another. Yet, people talk about probability casually, as though there is a widespread understanding of the term. In this chapter, I introduce a workable definition of probability.

12.1 Definition of Probability

For us, we are going to think of the probability of an event as *the long run proportion of the occurrence of the event.*

So, what does this mean? Let's imagine that we consider flipping a coin and the event of interest is that the coin falls heads which we denote by the symbol H. Here, we introduce notation where P stands for probability, and we conveniently write the probability that the coin falls heads as

$$P(H).$$

In this example, when we talk about the long run proportion of heads, imagine that we flipped the coin many times; let's say 1,000 times. And, if we observed 519 heads, then the proportion of heads would be 519 occurrences divided by the 1,000 trials, leading to the observed proportion, $519/1000 = 0.519$. This proportion is sometimes expressed as the percentage, 51.9%.

Now, instead of 1,000 flips, imagine that we flipped the coin 50,000 times and observed 25,400 heads. Then, the observed proportion of heads would be 25,400 occurrences divided by the 50,000 trials, $25400/50000 = 0.508$, which as a percentage is 50.8%.

However, using the definition of probability given above, we do not have a fixed number of flips. Alternatively, we refer to the probability of heads P(H) as the *long run proportion* of heads. That is, we do not flip the coin 1,000 times, nor 50,000 times, but *we imagine* flipping the coin infinitely often. Now, infinity is a very very big number, much much larger than 50,000. Actually, infinity is a theoretical concept which we will not discuss. But I hope you have an intuition that with an infinite number of flips, we would end up with the following:

$$P(H) = 1/2 = 0.5.$$

In other words, the percentage of heads is exactly 50%.

A problem with defining probability like this is that we cannot flip the coin an infinite number of times in real life. In practice, we cannot do anything infinitely often. Therefore, even though we might believe that the assignment P(H) = 0.5 is perfectly reasonable, in general, the assignment of probabilities is a problematic task. In this example, we arrive at the probability assignment P(H) = 0.5 from a symmetry argument, believing that heads and tails are physically symmetric and that they are the only possible outcomes from flipping a coin. Therefore, the probability of heads P(H) and the probability of tails P(T) should be the same, i.e. P(H) = P(T) = 0.5.

So, I hope that you have got that. When flipping a coin, the event heads is assigned probability 1/2, and we interpret this as the proportion of heads that we would observe if we could flip the coin many, many times (i.e. infinitely often, although this is impossible in practice).

12.2 Probability in Pickleball

Let's relate the definition of probability to something practical in pickleball: a successful serve. What I mean by a successful serve is that your serve is in play; it neither goes into the net nor is out of bounds. For convenience we denote the probability as P(S) where S stands for a successful serve.

How are we to interpret P(S)? Using the definition of probability introduced in the first paragraph of Section 12.1, P(S) is the long run proportion of your serves that are successful. In other words, if you were to serve many, many times (i.e. infinitely often), P(S) is the proportion of your serves that are successful.

Immediately, you can see that there is a difficulty. Even though we can interpret P(S), what is the numerical value that ought to be assigned to this probability? In this case, we cannot make an appeal to symmetry like we did with the coin that had two physically identical sides (i.e. heads and tails).

The best that we can do is assign a numerical value for P(S) that estimates the true probability based on observed data. For example, you may have a friend who watches you play many pickleball matches, and records both your number of successful serves s and the total number of serves T. You might then assign the estimate P(S) = s/T.

A less attractive option may assign a numerical value to P(S) based on a guess. Of course, a guess should have some basis in reality - for example, maybe the guess is the same as an estimate for a comparable player. It may also be possible to assign an interval of values corresponding to P(S). For example, maybe you have strong intuition that the numerical value for P(S) lies somewhere in the interval between 0.70 and 0.95. In this case, when determining optimal strategies, you could do a sensitivity analysis using a range of plausible values, say P(S) = 0.70, 0.75, 0.80, 0.85, 0.90, 0.95.

Clearly, there are many phenomena in pickleball where probabilities are of interest; e.g. the probability of executing a third shot drop, the probability of executing a successful lob, the probability of executing a serve that is an "ace", the probability of defeating an opponent, the probability of winning a tournament, etc.

Finally, it is worth noting that some probabilities are better estimated than others. For example, I don't lob very often, and I don't have a good feel for the success probability related to my lobs. Also, I have made the point that the probabilities are personal. For example, my probability of executing a successful serve is likely different from your probability of executing a successful serve. But there is more to it than that. Often, probabilities are also dependent on your opponent and this needs to be taken into consideration when

Chapter 12. Probability

assigning probabilities. For example, my probability of returning a serve depends on the player who is serving to me.

So, to summarize: whether something happens or not in pickleball, there is an associated probability. To develop strategies, you need to assign pickleball probabilities. You will not know these probabilities exactly. However, you likely have a feel for these probabilities. For example, you likely know whether your probability of returning a serve is closer to 0.7 or closer to 0.9. Your experience playing pickleball (or possibly by collecting data) will help you assign probabilities.

Ok, I hope that you have at least a general understanding of probability. Again, the probability of an event is viewed as its long run frequency of occurrence. And, in the practical applications involving probability (Chapters 13-15), you will need to estimate your personal probabilities. If you don't quite have it, maybe read Chapter 12 again. And if you still don't quite have it, that is ok. The idea will be illustrated with specific pickleball strategies in the following chapters.

CHAPTER 13

Letting the Ball Go

This is the simplest example using the probability concepts outlined in Chapter 12. If you do not completely grasp everything, hang in there, and at the end of this chapter, you will find some specific advice. This may help improve your game.

I am interested in a common pickleball problem that requires that you make a decision. It concerns a shot that is hit to you a little bit high, is hit with speed and is challenging. There is a chance that the ball may go out of bounds. Should you hit it or should you get out of the way and hope that it lands out of bounds?

Now, amongst some players, there is a tendency to often hit the ball, even if it would have gone out of bounds. Hitting the ball may simply be an automatic reaction and not involve any active strategic thinking. Alternatively, the decision to hit the ball could be motivated by psychological regret. Some people feel that if they let a ball go that lands in bounds, then they have lost the rally without providing a proper fight. They hate this possibility, and therefore, they tend to hit a lot of balls that are high and hard. However, this sentiment is not based on an analytics perspective; one should view the problem of letting the ball go using a probabilistic framework.

Accordingly, let's try to utilize the concepts from Chapter 12 where we begin by introducing some notation. Let $P(OB)$ denote the probability that the ball fired near you goes out of bounds if

Chapter 13. Letting the Ball Go

left untouched. Of course, as the ball is hit towards you, you don't know for sure whether it will be in bounds or out of bounds; that is why there is an associated probability. Also, the ball is hit to you very quickly and you obviously do not have time to assess the probability of the shot landing out of bounds based on its speed and its trajectory. Later, I suggest some heuristics that will assist you in making good assessments regarding the probability P(OB).

Following the development in Chapter 12, we want to calculate the probability of winning the rally given that the ball has been hit hard towards you and is challenging. Recall that probability is a long run proportion; in other words, it is the proportion of time that you would win the rally had the same circumstance been repeated over and over again. And winning the rally is the relevant criterion - this is ultimately what is most important in making pickleball decisions.

Now, we want to calculate the probability of winning the rally under two scenarios; under strategy H (you hit the ball), and under strategy G (you let the ball go). If the probability of winning the rally under strategy G is greater than the probability of winning the rally under strategy H, then your optimal decision is to let the ball go. In the long run, you will do better under strategy G if its win probability is greater.

Let's first calculate the probability of winning the rally $P_H(\text{Win})$ under strategy H (you hit the ball). Note that I have introduced the subscript "H" to emphasize strategy H. Since the ball has been hit hard and is challenging to handle, we will assume that you are going to win this rally less than 50% of the time. In other words, we are going to make the assumption

$$P_H(\text{Win}) < 0.5 .$$

Chapter 13. Letting the Ball Go

Again, we have assessed that on average, you will win the rally less than 50% of the time when you hit a challenging and hard hit ball. I think this probability assignment is reasonable; in an evenly contested match, once the first couple of shots have been played and the serve effect is diminished, you are going to win a rally roughly 50% of the time. In this circumstance, since the ball is hit hard and is challenging, you are at a disadvantage, and therefore the value should be less than 50%.

Now, let's calculate the probability of winning the rally $P_G(\text{Win})$ under strategy G (you let the ball go). When you let the ball go, the only way you can win the rally is if the ball goes out of bounds. Therefore, we have

$$P_G(\text{Win}) = P(\text{OB}) \,.$$

We now put this all together and provide some helpful advice. We want to compare the probability $P_H(\text{Win})$ of winning the rally under strategy H (you hit the ball) with the probability $P_G(\text{Win})$ of winning the rally under strategy G (you let the ball go). Since $P_H(\text{Win}) < 0.5$, the probability $P_G(\text{Win})$ is greater whenever

$$P_G(\text{Win}) = P(\text{OB}) > 0.5 \,. \tag{13.1}$$

In other words, from equation (13.1), strategy G (you let the ball go) is preferable whenever $P(\text{OB}) > 0.5$.

Therefore, and this is the most important piece of advice that you need to remember from this chapter: let the challenging and hard hit ball go if there is greater than a 50% chance that it will land out of bounds.

Now, in the midst of a game, with the ball flying towards you,

Chapter 13. Letting the Ball Go

how can you possibly make a probability calculation to determine whether you should let the ball go? It is impossible.

Therefore, I want to make the advice a little more tangible. I have collected some data on fast shots that are challenging and a bit high as illustrated in Figure 13.1. The reported estimated probabilities P(OB) are based on a variety of shots that are similar to those depicted in the diagram. It is actually difficult to collect such data and to reliably estimate probabilities P(OB). Estimation is difficult because real-life pickleball shots vary in so many ways. The wind, the speed of the shot and the trajectory of the shot are obviously very important components that impact P(OB). Also, the location of the sender and the receiver on the court are also important and affect P(OB). For example, if the receiver is positioned near the endline, then any shot that passes the receiver in the air will naturally land out of bounds if the receiver lets it go. That is, P(OB) = 1.0 if the receiver is at the endline.

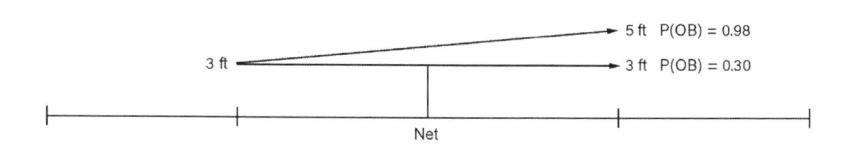

Figure 13.1: Estimated probabilities P(OB) of shots going out of bounds under two scenarios as the ball is hit from the left side to the right side of the court. A probability exceeding 0.5 corresponds to a shot that the receiver should let go.

Chapter 13. Letting the Ball Go

Figure 13.1 provides a specific and simplified[1] illustration. Note that both the sender and receiver are located in the middle of their side of the court. You may also consider other scenarios. Further, I am assuming that the sender's shots are reasonably fast. What I mean by this is that the sender takes a good swing at the ball. For example, it is not a block shot nor is it a lob. Of course, some players hit the ball harder than other players, and therefore, such issues need to be taken into consideration. In Figure 13.1, I am particularly concerned about the reliability of the P(OB) estimate in the case where the height of the ball is 3.0 feet at the sender's location and is 3.0 feet at the receiver's location. I consider the estimate P(OB) = 0.30 in this instance as an upper bound. That is, the true value is no larger than P(OB) = 0.30.

When you see P(OB) > 0.5 in Figure 13.1, this is a situation where you should let the ball go (i.e. don't try to hit it). In this situation, letting the ball go is a better strategy than hitting the ball.

Taking all of the caveats into consideration, you should be able to develop some personal heuristics to decide when to let the ball go. For example, you might decide that if you are in the middle of your half of the court and the ball comes whizzing by at 3 feet high or lower, you ought to hit it. If however, it is five feet high or higher, certainly let it go since P(OB) > 0.5. For some of you, the benchmark for letting the ball go might be shoulder height, something easy to remember. The difficult decisions occur in the intermediate

---

[1] Gravity does not allow us to hit the pickleball in straight lines as shown in Figure 13.1. Rather, the path will have an arc that slightly resembles the symbol "⌒". Therefore, you may prefer to interpret Figure 13.1 as follows: if the ball is hit from height x feet, crosses the net at height y feet and approaches the opponent at height z feet, then x and z are correct but the true y value is a little larger than shown, creating the desired arc.

Chapter 13. Letting the Ball Go

range, say when the ball passes at a height between 3.0 feet and 5.0 feet. What is the true probability P(OB) in those cases? Again, it depends on many factors including the wind, ball speed, the ball trajectory and your positioning on the court. It is only through thoughtful experience that you will develop solid heuristics.

Let's summarize the two main takeaways from this chapter:

- The concise suggestion in this chapter is to let a challenging and hard hit ball go if the ball has at least a 50% chance of landing out of bounds. The novelty in this advice is the 50% threshold. Many players believe that you need to be correct far more often than 50% of the time. However, analytics suggests that you will be better off in the long run (i.e. win more rallies) if you adopt the 50% criterion. The paradox is partly explained by recognizing that you will still lose rallies if you decide to play the ball.

- My experience is that many mid-level players attempt to return high and hard hit balls too frequently. Let some of them go and you will likely improve your pickleball results. Better yet, develop some simple personal heuristics as to when you should let the ball go. What I would do is create two simple rules: Rule #1 - When I am standing at the non-volley zone, I will let challenging and hard hit balls go that are x feet or higher. Rule #2 - When I am standing roughly in the middle of the court, I will let challenging and hard hit balls go that are y feet or higher. It is your job to determine your personal values for x and y.

Chapter 14

The Serve

When you are serving, there are many variations of a serve that are at your disposal. For example, you can introduce spin, speed and arc, and you can also vary the intended placement location. This chapter concerns the assessment of your various serving strategies.

I want to compare two serving strategies. We will denote the first serving strategy by C which stands for cautious. This is a serve for which you are confident. The serve is nearly always hit within the serving boundaries. It tends to land in the middle of the serving area and is not hit too hard. Recall from Chapter 4 that there is a prominent school of thought that you should always keep your serve in play.

The second serving strategy involves a "trickier" serve for your opponents to handle. We denote a particular tricky style as strategy T (for tricky). Although your opponents may be able to return your tricky serve, the intention is that it causes them a greater challenge than your cautious serve when it is executed correctly. Note that you may want to assess additional serving strategies from your arsenal of tricky serves. However, if you can follow the logic of comparing two strategies probabilistically (as will be done here), it is a simple matter to carry out comparisons involving additional serving strategies.

At this point, I am going to dig into probability derivations for

Chapter 14. The Serve

a while. If you would like to skip the technical details, you may fast forward to Section 14.1 for some practical results.

First, we are interested in the probability $P_C(\text{Win})$ of winning the rally using the cautious serving strategy C where we have introduced the subscript C for "cautious". To calculate this probability, we need to consider all the possible outcomes that can occur when the cautious serve is utilized. Accordingly, the strategy C may result in a serve that either lands in bounds or goes out of play (i.e. into the net or out of bounds). We are going to make the simplifying assumption that such a serve lands in bounds 100% of the time. Although false, I think this assumption is nearly true; recall that we described C as a strategy corresponding to a cautious serve for which the server has great confidence involving placement. Second, we are going to assume that the two teams are roughly evenly matched. If this is the case, the receiving team has an advantage during the rally. This is because the receiving team has the first opportunity to approach the non-volley zone (after the second shot), and it is a tenet of pickleball that this is a primary playing objective. We therefore write

$$P_C(\text{Win}) = x < 0.5 \, . \tag{14.1}$$

Now, we don't know the value of x, the probability of winning the rally using a cautious serve. But we do know that because the serving team is at a disadvantage involving two comparable teams, $x < 0.5$. I have done some counting in a small set of balanced pickleball matches, and I estimate that x lies somewhere in the interval $(0.35, 0.45)$. However, depending on your particular circumstances, you may prefer to replace x in (14.1) with a value that you believe is a better representation of your situation.

For the tricky serving strategy T, we need to calculate $P_T(\text{Win})$

which is the probability of winning the rally using serving strategy T. Here the subscript T is used to denote the tricky strategy under consideration. Hence, we have two probabilities of interest, $P_C(\text{Win})$ and $P_T(\text{Win})$ which are the probabilities of winning the rally under the two strategies. Once we are able to calculate these probabilities, we will compare them to see which is the larger. The larger probability will correspond to the preferred strategy.

For the calculation of $P_T(\text{Win})$, we first need to consider all of the possible outcomes that are associated with T. Under serving strategy T, there are three outcomes associated with the served ball:

- it may hit the net or land out of bounds (OB)
- it may land in bounds at an unintended location (IBU)
- it may land in bounds at the intended location (IBI)

To assess strategy T, we need to obtain the probability $P_T(\text{Win})$ of winning the rally using strategy T, taking into account the three possible outcomes associated with the tricky serve. We write

$$\begin{aligned} P_T(\text{Win}) &= P_T(\text{Win} \mid \text{OB})\, P_T(\text{OB}) \\ &+ P_T(\text{Win} \mid \text{IBU})\, P_T(\text{IBU}) \\ &+ P_T(\text{Win} \mid \text{IBI})\, P_T(\text{IBI}) \end{aligned} \quad (14.2)$$

where the expression (14.2) has three components corresponding to the three aforementioned outcomes.

Before addressing the components in equation (14.2), I need to introduce a new concept known as *conditional probability*. Conditional probability is still probability but it is used when additional information is revealed. For example, suppose a die is rolled - what is the probability that the die lands "1"? Since there are six faces

Chapter 14. The Serve

on the die and the die is symmetric, it is immediate that the probability is given by $P(1) = 1/6$. However, suppose I was to tell you in advance that the outcome from the roll of the die is an odd number, namely 1, 3 or 5. This is additional information, and we need to incorporate this information in the probability calculation. We write this new probability as $P(1 \mid \text{odd})$. With this notation, we are interested in the probability that a "1" occurs *given* that the outcome is odd. Here, the "|" sign is verbalized as "given" and what follows the sign is the additional information that impacts the probability. In this example, $P(1 \mid \text{odd}) = 1/3$ since "1" is one of the three possible symmetric outcomes 1, 3, 5.

Now, have a look at equation (14.2). There is new and related notation that has been introduced. For example, $P_T(\text{Win} \mid \text{IBU})$ is the conditional probability of winning the rally under strategy T given a serve with outcome IBU. That is, assuming that outcome IBU has occurred, $P_T(\text{Win} \mid \text{IBU})$ is the probability of winning the rally.

If you have not previously worked with probability, equation (14.2) may be puzzling. But we need to calculate equation (14.2); it is the crucial element in our comparison of the tricky serving strategy T versus the cautious serving strategy C. Remember, that when you are attempting the tricky serve, there are three possible outcomes (listed in the bullet points above) that can occur as a result of T. These three outcomes and their associated probabilities are expressed in the three lines of equation (14.2). In order to calculate the probability $P_T(\text{Win})$ of winning the rally with the tricky serving strategy, we need to assign the component probabilities associated with the three outcomes. These component probabilities (the six probabilities in equation (14.2)) each have precise meaning.

Because they have precise meaning, it is not that difficult for us to provide some plausible values for these probabilities according to our personal pickleball characteristics. In the next paragraph, I am going to explain how we go about assigning reasonable numerical values to the six probabilities in equation (14.2). This is detailed, but if you take your time, I know that you can absorb it.

Let's now work on providing numerical values for the entries in equation (14.2). First, it is impossible to win the rally if your serve goes out of bounds; this implies that $P_T(\text{Win} \mid \text{OB}) = 0$, and therefore, the first term in equation (14.2) can be ignored. Let's now assume that when you hit a ball in bounds but at an unintended location (i.e. outcome IBU), then the result is not much different than when utilizing the cautious serving strategy C. That is, the tricky serve was mishit in some way and is not as good as you hoped; it is probably similar to a cautious serve. This implies that $P_T(\text{Win} \mid \text{IBU}) = x$ which is taken from equation (14.1). Here, x is presumably a conservative estimate of $P_T(\text{Win} \mid \text{IBU})$; the true value is most likely a little larger than x. Next, there is the question of how much better is your tricky serve T than your cautious serve C when both are properly executed. Let's say it is 10% better; in other words, $P_T(\text{Win} \mid \text{IBI}) = x + 0.10$. We are going to actually be a little more general, and consider the tricky serve T to be better than C by a quantity y; i.e. $P_T(\text{Win} \mid \text{IBI}) = x + y$. We are going to make one final assumption; I think it is reasonable to assume that your tricky serve that lands in bounds but is hit to an unintended location (IBU) will occur at roughly the same rate that your tricky serve T goes out of bounds (OB). Both of these are badly executed serves. In other words, we assume $P_T(\text{IBU}) = P_T(\text{OB})$. Now, together with the fact that $P_T(\text{IBU}) + P_T(\text{OB}) + P_T(\text{IBI}) = 1$, some

Chapter 14. The Serve

simple algebra gives $P_T(\text{IBU}) = (1 - P_T(\text{IBI}))/2$. Putting all of these pieces together, equation (14.2) reduces to

$$P_T(\text{Win}) = (x/2 + y) \, P_T(\text{IBI}) + x/2 \, . \tag{14.3}$$

Hang in. We are nearly there. Recall the logic is that the tricky serving strategy T is better than the cautious serving strategy C if $P_T(\text{Win}) > P_C(\text{Win})$. This means that the tricky serve is the superior strategy if

$$P_T(\text{Win}) - P_C(\text{Win}) > 0 \, .$$

Therefore, we substitute equations (14.1) and (14.3) into the left hand side of the above displayed equation. Doing so, we conclude that the tricky serve is better than the cautious serve when

$$P_T(\text{Win}) - P_C(\text{Win}) = (x/2 + y) \, P_T(\text{IBI}) - x/2 \tag{14.4}$$

exceeds zero.

The evaluation of (14.4) is not difficult. In Table 14.1, I calculate equation (14.4) for plausible combinations of x, y and $P_T(\text{IBI})$. When equation (14.4) exceeds zero, then the tricky serve T is preferable to the cautious serve C.

To recap, what is important is that you have a good understanding of the meaning of x, y and $P_T(\text{IBI})$. These are the characteristics related to your serves. If you get a handle on these quantities, you can then assess your serving strategy T compared to your serving strategy C via equation (14.4).

Now, what I am going to do is suggest some values of x, y and $P_T(\text{IBI})$ that may be plausible. In Table 14.1, we select two values for

Chapter 14. The Serve

consideration, $x = 0.35$ and $x = 0.45$ corresponding to the success rate of the cautious serve which we know should be less than 0.5. For the input setting y, we consider two moderate values, $y = 0.05$ and $y = 0.15$ which correspond to the amount that the tricky serve T is better than the cautious serve C when they are both executed successfully. If your tricky serve is no better than your cautious serve when executed properly, there would be no sense in even considering the tricky serve. For the tricky serve, we are going to further assume that you are going to be able to hit it in bounds at the intended location more often than not. We are going to select two values, $P_T(IBI) = 0.60, 0.90$ which both exceed 1/2. Again, you would not even consider a tricky serve unless you can execute it frequently. This leads to a total of $2(2)(2) = 8$ combinations of plausible settings given in Table 14.1.

x	y	P_T(IBI)	Eqn (14.4)
0.35	0.05	0.60	-0.0400
0.35	0.05	0.90	0.0275
0.35	0.15	0.60	0.0200
0.35	0.15	0.90	0.1175
0.45	0.05	0.60	-0.0600
0.45	0.05	0.90	0.0225
0.45	0.15	0.60	0.0000
0.45	0.15	0.90	0.1225

Table 14.1: Calculation of equation (14.4) for plausible values of x, y and P_T(IBI). When the quantity exceeds zero, it suggests that the tricky serve T is preferable to the cautious serve C.

14.1 Some Practical Results

So, if you have struggled with the probability derivations, you can now begin to read seriously. The main takeaway from Table 14.1 is that most settings give positive values for equation (14.4). This implies that the tricky serve is almost always better than the cautious serve. The only times when the cautious serve is better corresponds to the case where $P_T(\text{IBI}) = 0.60$. The bottom line is that your tricky serve is preferable if you can hit it where you want it to go more than 60% of the time. That doesn't seem so hard to do? Note that this advice seems to contradict prevailing pickleball wisdom. Moreover, the value y greatly impacts equation (14.4). If you have a killer serve in your back pocket that is much better than your cautious serve (i.e. large y), you should use it.

There is another instructional aspect regarding the entries in Table 14.1. Suppose, for example, that the fourth row in Table 14.1 corresponds closely to the characteristics of your serves. That is, $P_T(\text{Win}) - P_C(\text{Win}) = 0.1175$. This allows us to interpret the two serves; it states that your tricky serve wins the rally 11.75% more often than the cautious serve. However, we can also use equations (14.3) and (14.1) to calculate the components $P_T(\text{Win})$ and $P_C(\text{Win})$. Under the settings leading to the fourth row in Table 14.1, $P_T(\text{Win}) = 0.4675$ and $P_C(\text{Win}) = 0.35$. This means that your tricky serve wins the point 46.75% of the time and your cautious serve wins the point 35.0% of the time. The approach described above permits interpretability of the success rate of your personal strategies.

Finally, we have stated previously that the proposed probabilistic approach allows the pickleballer to identify areas for personal improvement. To illustrate, suppose that row 7 of Table 14.1 reasonably represents your game. In this case, your cautious serve and your tricky serve are the same in terms of winning rallies. However, what differs from line 7 to line 8 in Table 14.1 is that your probability of hitting the tricky serve in bounds at the intended location goes up from 60% to 90% of the time (third column). If you can achieve this increased level of accuracy, your improvement in winning rallies with the tricky serve will increase dramatically by 12.25% (fourth column).

Chapter 15

The Third Shot Drop

This chapter concerns a comparison of the third shot drop versus a third shot drive.

A common and challenging situation arises in pickleball when you are on the serving team. Suppose that you have served and the receiving team has made a deep return. They have also advanced to the edge of their non-volley zone (NVZ). You are therefore in a vulnerable position. You are quite far back, and your opponents are ready to attack. There are not too many viable options available to you.

In this context, the most highly recommended strategy for your third shot is the famous "third shot drop". This is a soft shot where your intention is to just clear the net and land your shot in the opponent's NVZ. The objective is to avoid giving your opponents a volley shot and to slow the game down, giving you and your partner time to approach your NVZ. If this is done successfully, the game may enter the dinking phase. The third shot drop is a great strategy; unfortunately it is a difficult shot to master. It needs to be hit with precision. If it is hit too high, your opponents will slam the ball back at you, and if it is hit too softly, it will go into the net. The third shot drop becomes more demanding the farther you are from your NVZ. For notational purposes, we will denote the third shot drop shot strategy by D, for drop.

The other strategy which I would like to compare against D is a return shot that is hit hard. Some people call this shot a "drive". However, for a little excitement, we will denote this strategy by B which stands for "bang". Banging the ball is likely easier to execute than the third shot drop, and this is part of its appeal.

At this point, if you want to skip the technical details and get to the practical results, you may fast forward to Section 15.1.

Following the same approach as in Chapter 13 and Chapter 14, we are interested in comparing two probabilities, $P_D(\text{Win})$ and $P_B(\text{Win})$ corresponding to winning the rally when using the third drop shot strategy and winning the rally when using the banging strategy, respectively. If $P_B(\text{Win}) > P_D(\text{Win})$, banging would be the preferred strategy, and this would be quite an unexpected result given the invective directed at banging and the adoration given to the third shot drop.

For the third shot drop strategy D, we need to consider all of the possible outcomes associated with D. Under strategy D, the three most common outcomes are:

- the drop is executed flawlessly (F)

- the drop results in the ball being hit in the net (N)

- the drop is hit too high (H)

There are actually more outcomes associated with D than the three outcomes listed above. However, the remaining outcomes can be ignored since they all occur with negligible probability (e.g. trying to hit a third shot drop but it ends up going long and out of bounds).

To assess strategy D, we need to obtain the probability $P_D(\text{Win})$ of winning the rally under D, taking into account the three possible outcomes associated with D. As in Chapter 14, we make use of

Chapter 15. The Third Shot Drop

conditional probability and write

$$\begin{aligned}P_D(\text{Win}) &= P_D(\text{Win} \mid \text{F}) \, P_D(\text{F}) \\ &+ P_D(\text{Win} \mid \text{N}) \, P_D(\text{N}) \\ &+ P_D(\text{Win} \mid \text{H}) \, P_D(\text{H}) \end{aligned} \qquad (15.1)$$

where equation (15.1) has three components corresponding to the three aforementioned outcomes.

Let's see if we can make some progress by simplifying equation (15.1). First, the easy part - if you hit the ball into the net (N), you lose the rally. Therefore, we have the conditional probability $P_D(\text{Win} \mid \text{N}) = 0$. Second, I would like to argue that if you flawlessly execute the third shot drop (F), both teams will then have approached the NVZ, and in principle, they will be on an equal footing. Then, the outcome of the rally between two evenly matched teams should be nearly a toss-up. We can express this notion by setting $P_D(\text{Win} \mid \text{F}) = 0.5$. Third, if you hit the third shot drop D too high (H), you have certainly given your opponents an advantage, and they are more likely to win the rally. For sure, $P_D(\text{Win} \mid \text{H}) < 0.5$. I don't have really good intuition on the probability $P_D(\text{Win} \mid \text{H})$, and I have not collected any relevant data. The conditional probability $P_D(\text{Win} \mid \text{H})$ will certainly depend on the quality of your opponent. However, for the analysis, let's try two plausible values, $P_D(\text{Win} \mid \text{H}) = 0.1$ and $P_D(\text{Win} \mid \text{H}) = 0.4$. Note that by hitting a high shot H, you have hit a poor shot, and therefore $P_D(\text{Win} \mid \text{H})$ should be certainly less than 0.5.

As for the remaining probabilities $P_D(\text{F})$, $P_D(\text{N})$ and $P_D(\text{H})$ in equation (15.1), these are personal probabilities and vary according to your personal skill level. What we may be willing to assume is that you make mistakes N and H at roughly the same rate such that $P_D(N) = P_D(H)$. And given that $P_D(F) + P_D(N) + P_D(H) = 1$, let's entertain the values $P_D(F) = 0.2, 0.8$ according to widely varying skill levels, and consequently set $P_D(N) = P_D(H) = (1 - P_D(F))/2$.

With the above argumentation, equation (15.1) simplifies to

$$P_D(\text{Win}) = P_D(F)/2 + P_D(\text{Win} \mid H)\,(1 - P_D(F))/2\,. \quad (15.2)$$

Now let's turn to the calculation of $P_B(\text{Win})$, the probability of winning the rally under the banging strategy. For simplicity, let's assume that only two outcomes can occur under strategy B:

- you hit the ball out of bounds which means left, right, long or into the net (OB)

- you hit a good banging shot (G); by good, I mean in the sense that the ball is in play

In a similar fashion to equation (15.1), we therefore write

$$\begin{aligned}P_B(\text{Win}) &= P_B(\text{Win} \mid \text{OB})\,P_B(\text{OB}) \\ &\quad + P_B(\text{Win} \mid G)\,P_B(G) \end{aligned} \quad (15.3)$$

where equation (15.3) has two components corresponding to the two outcomes associated with B.

We now wish to simplify equation (15.3). Since out of bounds shots (OB) result in lost rallies, this implies that $P_B(\text{Win} \mid \text{OB}) = 0$, and therefore, equation (15.3) becomes

$$P_B(\text{Win}) = P_B(\text{Win} \mid G)\,P_B(G)\,. \quad (15.4)$$

I suspect that the first term in equation (15.4) has many plausible

Chapter 15. The Third Shot Drop 103

values due to a wide range of player skill levels (both you and your opponent). We therefore consider two disparate values of $P_B(\text{Win} \mid G)$, specifically $P_B(\text{Win} \mid G) = 0.2$ and $P_B(\text{Win} \mid G) = 0.8$. Given a good banging shot, we are saying that the probability of winning the rally can vary greatly, from rarely winning (probability 0.2) to frequently winning (probability 0.8). For your execution in hitting the good banging shot, I would think you should be able to get the ball in play at least half the time. Otherwise, you would not even attempt the shot. Therefore, we consider two values, $P_B(G) = 0.6$ and $P_B(G) = 0.9$, noting that $P_B(G) \geq 0.5$ in both cases.

To assess the two strategies D and B, we use equations (15.2) and (15.4), and write

$$\begin{aligned} P_B(\text{Win}) - P_D(\text{Win}) &= P_B(\text{Win} \mid G)\, P_B(G) - P_D(F)/2 \\ &\quad - P_D(\text{Win} \mid H)\,(1 - P_D(F))/2\,. \end{aligned} \quad (15.5)$$

15.1 Some Practical Results

Recall that equation (15.5) is the key numerical score for comparison; when it exceeds zero, it provides evidence in favour of the drive (i.e. banging) over the third shot drop. When the value is less than zero, it provides evidence in favour of the third shot drop over the drive.

Equation (15.5) is evaluated under a range of 16 plausible conditions previously discussed. The results are shown in Table 15.1. Let's immediately get to the conclusion that everyone was expecting. It is this: if you can hit it well, the third shot drop is the preferred shot in the scenario when your team is back and the opponents have approached the NVZ. How do we see this probabilistically? Let's say you can hit the third shot drop really well, and for illustration,

Chapter 15. The Third Shot Drop

let's set $P_D(F) = 1$. Referring back to the notation, this means that you hit the third shot drop flawlessly all of the time. Of course, you can't, but let's say that you can get close to the desired skill level. We then substitute $P_D(F) = 1$ into equation (15.5). If you make the substitution, then equation (15.5) reduces to

$$P_B(\text{Win}) - P_D(\text{Win}) = P_B(\text{Win} \mid G)\, P_B(G) - 1$$

which is *always* negative[1].

This provides indisputable evidence of the importance of the third shot drop. The corollary is that you should practice the third shot drop so that you can execute it with a high success rate.

Now let's get into the weeds a bit, and consider the case where you don't actually hit the third shot drop all that well. Suppose you can only execute it 50% of the time (i.e. $P_D(F) = 0.5$). And let's also say that you are pretty good with the drive; that is, 50% of the time, your drive will result in winning the rally (i.e. $P_B(\text{Win} \mid G) = 0.5$). And let's reasonably assume that you can get your drive in play most of the time (i.e. $P_B(G) > 0.5$). Then, using equation (15.5), it may be surprising that the drive is preferable to the third shot drop.

Although there is widespread condemnation against banging (i.e. the drive), we see that the drive is good when you cannot hit the third shot drop well but your drive poses a challenging shot for your opponents to handle. However, it is also important to recognize that against better competitors, attempting to blast the ball by them will become a less successful strategy (i.e. $P_B(\text{Win} \mid G)$ will decrease).

One of the insights that can be taken from Table 15.1 and from

---
[1] The expression involves a probability $P_B(\text{Win} \mid G)$ multiplied by a probability $P_B(G)$. Since these probabilities are each less than 1, the product is less than 1. It then follows that $P_B(\text{Win} \mid G)\, P_B(G) - 1 < 0$.

further exploration with equation (15.5) is that players can investigate where their games need improvement. For example, there are meaningful improvements that can be achieved by improving the third shot drop (i.e. increasing the execution rate $P_D(F)$). With these tools, you can ask and answer questions such as how much better will I be if I can improve my third shot drop execution rate $P_D(F)$ from say 60% to 70%? Given some practice, this seems to be a reasonable goal. To answer the above question, all that you need to do is substitute your personal values into equation (15.5).

Ok, one final time, and allow me to package this a little bit differently: The famous third shot drop is a great shot to have in your pickleball toolkit. And this applies to the same degree for any drop shot executed under similar conditions, not just the third shot. However, you need to be able to hit that third shot drop well, at least 50% of the time. If you can't do that, I would say, go out there and practice your drop shots. If you can get the flawless execution of your drop shots up to 80%, this is really going to help your game (see Table 15.1).

$P_D(F)$	$P_D(\text{Win} \mid H)$	$P_B(G)$	$P_B(\text{Win} \mid G)$	Eqn (15.5)
0.2	0.1	0.6	0.2	-0.02
0.2	0.1	0.6	0.8	0.34
0.2	0.1	0.9	0.2	0.04
0.2	0.1	0.9	0.8	0.58
0.2	0.4	0.6	0.2	-0.14
0.2	0.4	0.6	0.8	0.22
0.2	0.4	0.9	0.2	-0.08
0.2	0.4	0.9	0.8	0.46
0.8	0.1	0.6	0.2	-0.29
0.8	0.1	0.6	0.8	0.07
0.8	0.1	0.9	0.2	-0.23
0.8	0.1	0.9	0.8	0.31
0.8	0.4	0.6	0.2	-0.32
0.8	0.4	0.6	0.8	0.04
0.8	0.4	0.9	0.2	-0.26
0.8	0.4	0.9	0.8	0.28

Table 15.1: Calculation of equation (15.5) for plausible values of $P_D(F)$, $P_D(\text{Win} \mid H)$, $P_B(G)$ and $P_B(\text{Win} \mid G)$. When the quantity exceeds zero, it suggests that banging is preferable to the third shot drop.

CHAPTER 16

Summary

Here are some of the general themes from the book that I have attempted to communicate:

(A) Listen to what people have to say. There is some good advice out there. But be critical and assess the extent that the advice applies to you. Maybe particular advice does not apply in all circumstances (e.g. advancing to the non-volley zone together). And advice does change over time; the sport of pickleball is evolving.

(B) There is a balance that needs to be struck between being cautious and being aggressive. When you are too cautious, you may be potentially giving up points that could be earned through a more aggressive approach. When you are too aggressive, you may be conceding points through unforced errors.

(C) Don't be predictable. You will know that you are predictable when your opponents start taking advantage of your tendencies. In this case, change your patterns once in a while.

(D) Know your game. What that means is be familiar with the probabilities of success with which you can hit different types of shots. Although more difficult, also try to know the games of your opponents and your partners. Even if you can only assign rough probabilities, then the methods of Part III can assist you in identifying plausible strategies. Collect data on your game to help assign probabilities; this is something you can trust. And as a byproduct of knowing your probabilities and how they effect strategy, you will know which parts of your game to target for improvement.

(E) If you really want to improve, reduce the rate that you make unforced errors (see Chapter 7).

(F) An overall message in the monograph concerns randomness. Randomness is present in many aspects of sport. If we knew for sure how matches were going to turn out, there would be no need to play and there would be little interest in matches. The random element makes sport fun and makes strategy relevant.

Made in the USA
Columbia, SC
18 December 2024